25 Management Strategies for Delhi Metro's success

The Sreedharan Way..

First Edition : April 2012

ISBN : 978-93-5067-449-9

Published by :
Anuj Dayal, Chief PRO, Delhi Metro Rail Corporation Ltd.
E-mail : anuj@delhimetrorail.com, anujdayal.dmrc@gmail.com
Website : www.delhimetrorail.com

Typeset, Designed & Printed by :
M/s National Advertising Agency
E-mail : naa.creative@gmail.com, naaindia@gmail.com
Website : www.nationaladagency.in

Contents

"When we are inspired by some great purpose,
some extraordinary project,
all your thoughts break their bounds.
Your mind transcends limitations, your consciousness
expands in every direction, and you find yourself
in a new, great & wonderful world.

Dormant forces, faculties and talents come alive,
and you discover yourself
to be a greater person by far than you ever
dreamt yourself to be."

Maharishi Patanjali,
YogaSutra (500 BC)

DELHI METRO

Preface

It gives me immense pleasure to introduce this book titled ***"25 Management Strategies for Delhi Metro's Success"*** before you. There have been number of stories written about Delhi Metro's success, its achievements and its milestones. However, so far the media and the general public have not been able to completely comprehend the list of ***'Management Strategies'*** followed at DMRC that made it click as an organization. This book is, therefore, a nice attempt to translate the philosophy and the strong work culture prevailing at DMRC since its inception that propels it to scale new heights each day.

The core values such as punctuality, integrity, professionalism and others that we strictly adhere to and which we practice religiously on a day-to-day basis find very apt description in different chapters of this book. In fact, these values essentially form the basis of our philosophy and work culture in Delhi Metro. Work culture, as we all know, requires a very disciplined and concentrated effort from the Management point of view that has to be inculcated in an individual right from the beginning. I think the efforts of Dr. E. Sreedharan have paid off well and we have been able to establish a system that sets us apart as an organization, that meets its targets and is committed to excellence and beyond in modern India.

Constructing the Metro in the capital of the country amidst maddening traffic and a huge population had its own share of hurdles and obstacles to confront with ranging from litigations arising out of land acquisitions, shop/market demolition & its relocation, paying compensation to the affected private parties, tree cutting and environmental clearance, permissions required for utility diversion and others. Each of these problems is, actually, a case study from the management perspective. The chapters pertaining to the above topics in this book and the efficient management strategies that the DMRC adopted in mitigating those problems gives a rare insight to the proactive approach and out-of-the box thinking of the DMRC engineers/managers.

I would like to compliment Mr. Anuj Dayal, Chief Public Relations Officer and his editorial team for coming out with such a wonderful publication which has been brought out in a very simple and straightforward manner.

Mangu Singh
Managing Director
Delhi Metro Rail Corporation (DMRC)

Overview

The fundamental secret for successful project execution is to ensure that the project is completed within the budget and the time frame specified. Time is money and the moment a project is delayed, the cost of the project shoots up automatically because of inflation. To avoid this, it is necessary to have a quick decision making process in the organization.

The hurdles which an infrastructure project encounters include difficulties in land acquisition, permission required for tree cutting and adequate funding. In addition, it is very necessary to have a technically competent team in position to tackle complex engineering problems encountered during the project execution.

190 kms of a Modern Metro

The Delhi Metro Rail Corporation has constructed one of the most modern Metro Rail systems in the capital city of Delhi and the national capital region covering one hundred and ninety kilometers in only twelve years time. The construction of the first phase began on the 1st of October 1998 and the first section of 8.3 kilometers between Shahdara and Tis Hazari was inaugurated on 24th December 2002. Since then, DMRC began extending the Metro network by opening new sections almost in every six months till the network spread to 190 kilometers in 2011. This network now consists of seven lines with the Red Line covering 24 kilometers running between Dilshad Garden and Rithala, Yellow Line covering 47 kilometers running between Jahangirpuri and HUDA City Centre, Blue Line covering 49 kilometers between Dwarka Sector 21 and Noida City Centre with a branch line covering 9 kilometers between Yamuna Bank and Vaishali, Green Line covering 15 kilometers from Inderlok to Mundka and Kirti Nagar, Violet Line covering 20 kilometers running between Central Secretariat and Badarpur and the Orange Airport Express Line covering 23 kilometers from New Delhi to Dwarka Sector 21.

In a country where many projects especially in the government sector, are plagued by cost and time overruns, the DMRC managed to complete Phase I of the project two years and nine months ahead of schedule and Phase II was done in a record time of only four and a half years to meet the Commonwealth Games deadline. The two phases were constructed within cost and without causing any environmental damage to the city as the DMRC agreed for compensatory afforestation of planting ten trees for every tree cut by it during the construction. In addition, the Corporation took care of public sensibilities by diverting all water, sewer, electric and telephone lines in advance so that the public was not affected during the Metro construction. All the city roads were kept clear around the Metro construction areas and roads were widened in advance by DMRC around their

DELHI METRO

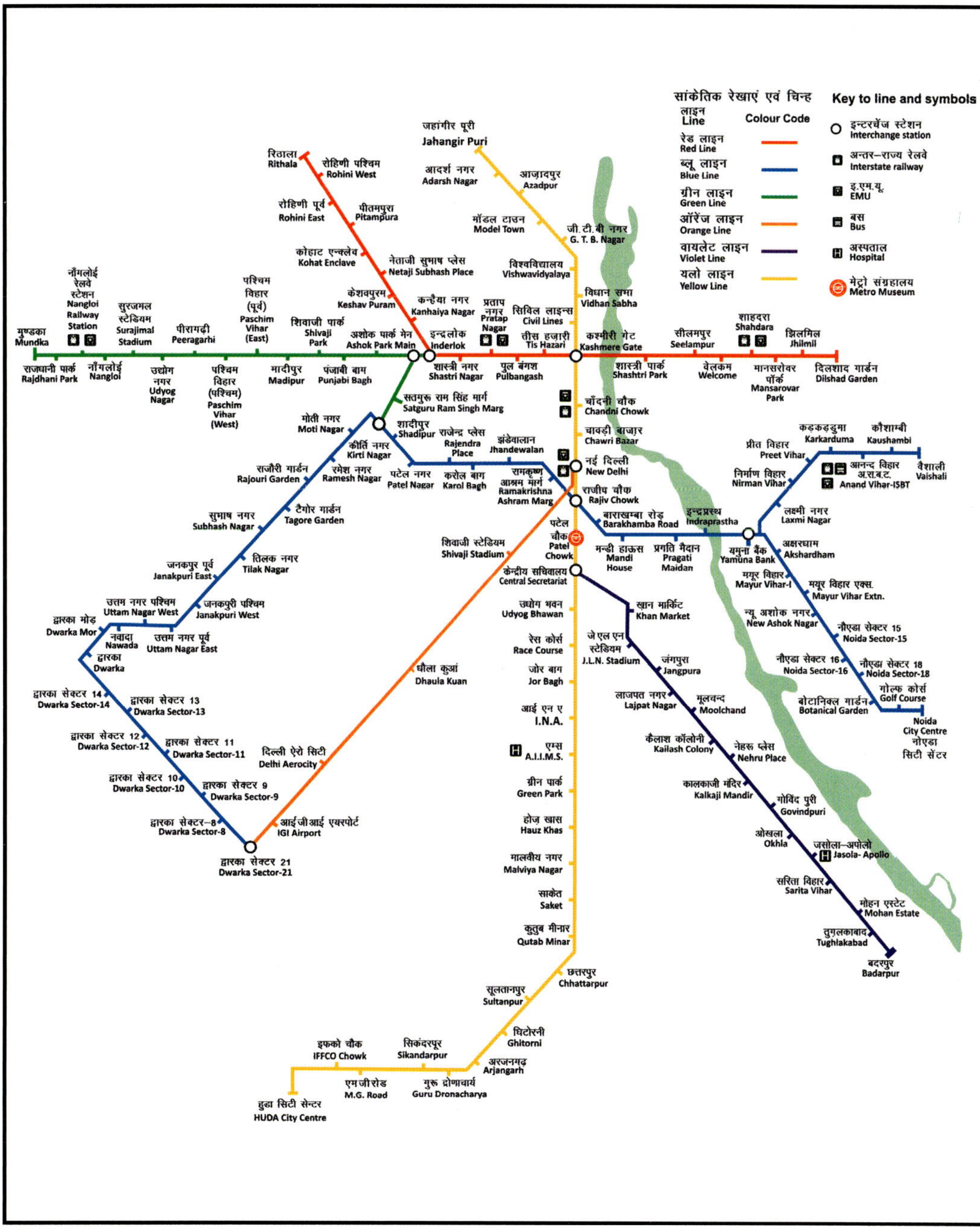

सांकेतिक रेखाएं एवं चिन्ह
Key to line and symbols
लाइन Line
Colour Code
रेड लाइन Red Line
ब्लू लाइन Blue Line
ग्रीन लाइन Green Line
ऑरेंज लाइन Orange Line
वायलेट लाइन Violet Line
यलो लाइन Yellow Line
इन्टरचेंज स्टेशन Interchange station
अन्तर–राज्य रेलवे Interstate railway
इ.एम.यू. EMU
बस Bus
अस्पताल Hospital
मेट्रो संग्रहालय Metro Museum
रिठाला Rithala
रोहिणी पश्चिम Rohini West
रोहिणी पूर्व Rohini East
पीतमपुरा Pitampura
कोहाट एन्क्लेव Kohat Enclave
नेताजी सुभाष प्लेस Netaji Subhash Place
केशवपुरम Keshav Puram
कन्हैया नगर Kanhaiya Nagar
इन्द्रलोक Inderlok
शास्त्री नगर Shastri Nagar
प्रताप नगर Pratap Nagar
पुल बंगश Pulbangash
तीस हज़ारी Tis Hazari
कश्मीरी गेट Kashmere Gate
शास्त्री पार्क Shashtri Park
सीलमपुर Seelampur
वेलकम Welcome
शाहदरा Shahdara
मानसरोवर पॉर्क Mansarovar Park
झिलमिल Jhilmil
दिलशाद गार्डन Dilshad Garden
जहांगीर पूरी Jahangir Puri
आदर्श नगर Adarsh Nagar
आज़ादपुर Azadpur
मॉडल टाउन Model Town
जी.टी.बी नगर G. T. B. Nagar
विश्वविद्यालय Vishwavidyalaya
विधान सभा Vidhan Sabha
सिविल लाइन्स Civil Lines
चाँदनी चौक Chandni Chowk
चावड़ी बाज़ार Chawri Bazar
नई दिल्ली New Delhi
राजीव चौक Rajiv Chowk
पटेल चौक Patel Chowk
केन्द्रीय सचिवालय Central Secretariat
उद्योग भवन Udyog Bhawan
रेस कोर्स Race Course
जोर बाग Jor Bagh
आई एन ए I.N.A.
एम्स A.I.I.M.S.
ग्रीन पार्क Green Park
होज़ खास Hauz Khas
मालवीय नगर Malviya Nagar
साकेत Saket
कुतुब मीनार Qutab Minar
छत्तरपुर Chhattarpur
सूलतानपुर Sultanpur
घिटोरनी Ghitorni
अरजनगढ़ Arjangarh
गुरु द्रोणाचार्य Guru Dronacharya
सिकंदरपूर Sikandarpur
एमजीरोड M.G. Road
इफको चौक IFFCO Chowk
हुडा सिटी सेन्टर HUDA City Centre
मुण्डका Mundka
राजधानी पार्क Rajdhani Park
नाँगलोई रेलवे स्टेशन Nangloi Railway Station
नाँगलोई Nangloi
सुरजमल स्टेडियम Surajimal Stadium
उद्योग नगर Udyog Nagar
पीरागढ़ी Peeragarhi
पश्चिम विहार (पश्चिम) Paschim Vihar (West)
पश्चिम विहार (पूर्व) Paschim Vihar (East)
मादीपुर Madipur
शिवाजी पार्क Shivaji Park
पंजाबी बाग Punjabi Bagh
अशोक पार्क मेन Ashok Park Main
सतगुरू राम सिंह मार्ग Satguru Ram Singh Marg
मोती नगर Moti Nagar
शादीपुर Shadipur
कीर्ति नगर Kirti Nagar
राजेन्द्र प्लेस Rajendra Place
झंडेवालान Jhandewalan
पटेल नगर Patel Nagar
करोल बाग Karol Bagh
रामकृष्ण आश्रम मार्ग Ramakrishna Ashram Marg
राजौरी गार्डन Rajouri Garden
रमेश नगर Ramesh Nagar
टैगोर गार्डन Tagore Garden
सुभाष नगर Subhash Nagar
तिलक नगर Tilak Nagar
जनकपुर पूर्व Janakpuri East
जनकपुरी पश्चिम Janakpuri West
उत्तम नगर पश्चिम Uttam Nagar West
उत्तम नगर पूर्व Uttam Nagar East
द्वारका मोड़ Dwarka Mor
नवादा Nawada
द्वारका Dwarka
द्वारका सेक्टर 14 Dwarka Sector-14
द्वारका सेक्टर 13 Dwarka Sector-13
द्वारका सेक्टर 12 Dwarka Sector-12
द्वारका सेक्टर 11 Dwarka Sector-11
द्वारका सेक्टर 10 Dwarka Sector-10
द्वारका सेक्टर 9 Dwarka Sector-9
द्वारका सेक्टर–8 Dwarka Sector-8
द्वारका सेक्टर 21 Dwarka Sector-21
आईजीआई एयरपोर्ट IGI Airport
दिल्ली ऐरो सिटी Delhi Aerocity
धौला कुआं Dhaula Kuan
शिवाजी स्टेडियम Shivaji Stadium
बाराखम्बा रोड Barakhamba Road
मन्डी हाऊस Mandi House
प्रगति मैदान Pragati Maidan
इन्द्रप्रस्थ Indraprastha
यमुना बैंक Yamuna Bank
अक्षरधाम Akshardham
मयूर विहार Mayur Vihar-I
मयूर विहार एक्स. Mayur Vihar Extn.
न्यू अशोक नगर New Ashok Nagar
नौएडा सेक्टर 15 Noida Sector-15
नौएडा सेक्टर 16 Noida Sector-16
नौएडा सेक्टर 18 Noida Sector-18
बोटानिकल गार्डन Botanical Garden
गोल्फ कोर्स Golf Course
Noida City Centre नोएडा सिटी सेंटर
लक्ष्मी नगर Laxmi Nagar
निर्माण विहार Nirman Vihar
प्रीत विहार Preet Vihar
कड़कड़डूमा Karkarduma
कौशाम्बी Kaushambi
आनन्द विहार अ.रा.ब.ट. Anand Vihar-ISBT
वैशाली Vaishali
खान मार्किट Khan Market
जे एल एन स्टेडियम J.L.N. Stadium
जंगपुरा Jangpura
लाजपत नगर Lajpat Nagar
मूलचन्द Moolchand
कैलाश कॉलोनी Kailash Colony
नेहरू प्लेस Nehru Place
कालकाजी मंदिर Kalkaji Mandir
गोविंद पुरी Govindpuri
ओखला Okhla
जसोला–अपोलो Jasola- Apollo
सरिता विहार Sarita Vihar
मोहन एस्टेट Mohan Estate
तुग़लकाबाद Tughlakabad
बदरपुर Badarpur

construction sites to enable smooth flow of traffic. The Corporation was sensitive to the sensibilities of the citizens and respected the cultural and heritage structures of Delhi as extra care was taken to ensure their safety during the construction process by adopting special construction methods in consultation with the Archaeological Survey of India.

One of the reasons for the success of DMRC was the quick decision making process, with all power vested in the Managing Director of the Corporation who took all decisions about the Corporation, even though the Corporation came under the purview of two governments i.e. the central government represented by the Ministry of Urban Development and the Government of the National Capital Territory of Delhi. The two governments who are the equity holders and therefore the owners of the DMRC, are represented on the Board of Directors of DMRC but did not interfere in the day to day working of the Corporation, which thus enjoyed considerable autonomy in functioning. At the political level too, interference was absent and with the project receiving accolades from the public for delivery on time, the political support was visible irrespective of the political parties in power.

The DMRC faced a tough technical challenge once it decided to go in for a modern Metro rail system as it had to gather the latest technical data and knowledge from all the Metros internationally and the best systems available globally in the fields of Metro electrification, signaling, telecommunication, rolling stock (Trains), civil engineering etc. which were adopted for the construction & operation of the Metro in Delhi. The DMRC decided to adopt the latest technology in every area and in some areas such as the automatic fare collection system and the Delhi Metro became the first Metro system globally to introduce a completely contact less token system for single journeys. The result was that the city of Delhi today has one of the most modern and advanced Metro systems internationally as the DMRC took advantage of the fact that it came late onto the Metro Scenario by going in for the latest technology.

The management style adopted by DMRC is another subject of interest to all those visitors who come to DMRC as they want to understand the methods and techniques adopted by the organisation to make all this happen. The DMRC adopted a practical approach based upon the experiences of their first Managing Director who had over 50 years of working experience. The technique and experience of Dr. Sreedharan are clearly reflected in the management systems adopted by DMRC which are elaborated in the subsequent chapters of this book.

Another important feature responsible for the success of this project was the careful handling of the legal aspects and litigations which could have been a big hindrance in project implementation as even a small chunk of land, if not acquired, could have delayed the whole project. Hundreds of cases went to the Courts/Judiciary at all levels right upto the Supreme Court against land acquisition as many owners were not keen to part with their land for natural reasons. However, the Courts of Law were very sympathetic to the project as they realized that it was for the public good as the city desperately needed a good, fast and efficient transport system since the roads were congested and the city was threatened with high levels of pollution caused by road vehicles. The legal wing of DMRC played a pivotal role in monitoring and briefing the judiciary at all times during the project stage thus ensuring that there were no delays caused on this account.

The team of people who were actually able to make the dream of a Metro in the capital city of India, Delhi, a reality were almost entirely drawn from the Government of India itself from departments like Railways largely initially, as Metro is also a rail based project and other departments like CPWD, Delhi Jal Board, Port Trust etc. chipped in later. The DMRC subsequently began to form its own cadre by recruiting personnel directly from the market through a competitive selection process. These groups of recruits from government backgrounds showed the nation that it was possible for people from the government to perform and deliver provided they were given the right opportunity and environment to function, both of which were available and provided by the management style adopted by the Delhi Metro Rail Corporation.

Metro Dream takes Birth

The population of the city of Delhi started increasing dramatically after the partition of India with the influx of a number of people from Pakistan into the capital of Delhi and the population doubled in 1947 itself as it increased from 0.6 million to 1.2 million. Today, the population of the city of Delhi has crossed 16 million and most of these people move by road.

The fact that more people can be moved by a rail based system was well known but it took time to realize the importance of movement by a rail based Mass Transit system within the city. London realized it in 1863 itself with the opening of a four mile network between Paddington (Bishop's Road) and Farringdon Street which today has grown to 413 kms and is the backbone of the city's transport system.

In Delhi, more than 35 studies were done on having a rail Based System but these studies remained on paper and did not fructify into a concrete project and therefore, did not become a reality. It was only in 1989 that the Government of Delhi decided to engage (Rail India Technical and Economic Service) RITES, a Government of India PSU under the Ministry of Railways to undertake a Detailed Project Report (DPR) to have a rail based transport system in the city of Delhi. Some amount of funding for this was given by the Ministry of Urban Development, Government of India since, the subject itself no longer came under the Ministry of Railways as the allocation of business rules was changed in 1986 as per which Metro Rail type transport within the city was allocated to the Ministry of Urban Development after the subject was transferred from the Railways. However, the only other Metro existing that time in India was in Kolkata, controlled and built by the Indian Railways. The construction in Kolkata began before 1976 when the subject was still with the Railways. The Kolkata Metro was built at a huge cost of ₹ 140 crs, the cost overrun was 12 times and the project, which was to be completed in the year 1980, was completed in 1996. It also disrupted city life in Kolkata very badly and some buildings collapsed during the construction. Kolkatans and their lives were greatly disturbed during the construction of Metro and the country was completely apprehensive about taking up any other Metro project in any other city. The Ministry of Railways continues to suffer financial losses on suburban sectors and no wonder the Railways were happy to have Metropolitan Rail Based transportation given to the Ministry of Urban Development, since they could not even raise fares due to domestic and political pressures faced in all suburban Rail systems throughout the country where they lose money. Railway suburban fares are a sensitive subject and often lead to anarchy and violence by suburban commuters, whenever an attempt is made to raise the fares for suburban travel.

Meanwhile, the Detailed Project Report in 1986 commissioned by the Delhi Government was finally completed in 1994 and was forwarded to the Ministry of Urban Development. The RITES report suggested a 55.3 kms network of Metro lines in the city of Delhi covering Delhi University-Central Secretariat, Shahdara-Barwala and Sabzi Mandi–Holambi Kalan. It was the Ministry of Urban Development under the then Secretary Mr. N.P. Singh, who subsequently vigorously began perusing this case. Mr. N.P. Singh, a Karnataka Cadre IAS officer, happened to know Mr. H.D.Deve Gowda, the then Prime Minister who had earlier been the Chief Minister of Karnataka. As a result of his efforts the Project was ultimately approved by the Government of India and the Japanese loan from the Japan Bank of International Cooperation (JBIC) (now called Japan International Corporation Agency, JICA) could be formalised and approved in 1995 while the Cabinet approval for the Project was received on 3rd May 1995 and the Delhi Metro Rail Corporation Ltd. was registered as a company with 50% equity participation from Government of Delhi and 50% from the Government of India.

This company was therefore, unique and different as no government has 51% or majority controlling shares in the company - as both had equal participation and therefore the Board of Directors of the company consisted of five representatives from the Government of India and five from the Government of Delhi with the Chairman of the company being appointed by the Government of India while the Managing Director is appointed by the Delhi Government. It was the Managing Director who was a full time appointee and would be in charge of the day to day running of this company. Today, the Board of Directors consist of sixteen representatives with six full time directors.

The Ministry of Urban Development then began a search to appoint an Assistant Company Secretary who could form the company and complete the formalities as per the Company Law. Mr. P.K.Gupta was the person selected as the Assistant Company Secretary based upon a newspaper advertisement to which he responded along with 20 other applicants. The seriousness of the appointment could be gauged from the fact that the interview board for this post was headed by the then Additional Secretary, Ministry of Urban Development, Mr. Hemendra Kumar and also had the Principal Secretary (Finance) of the Delhi Government as its member. Mr. Gupta joined as the first employee of the company on 4th April 1997 and two more persons joined soon after - Mrs. Saroj Rajwade, Financial Advisor and Chief Accounts Officer and Mr. D.D.Pahuja, Chief Electrical Engineer on deputation from the Indian Railways as the Government was keen to form a core team quickly. Meanwhile, the search for the most key position in the organisation namely the Managing Director was going on since the Japanese loan sanctioned in March 1997 had a condition that the company had to have a Managing Director in position, otherwise, there was the danger of the loan itself lapsing as a headless organisation would not inspire confidence in the Japanese Government about the project taking off. The search for the Managing Director was thus, going on and Mr. P.V.Jai Krishna, the then Chief Secretary of Delhi suggested the name of Dr. E. Sreedharan, who was then Chairman and Managing Director of the Konkan Railway Corporation. Mr. Jai Krishna had already seen the working of Dr. Sreedharan when he was Secretary in Goa during the construction of the Konkan Railway and was impressed by his performance. Unfortunately, Dr. Sreedharan was already 65 years of age and had passed the accepted retirement age of 58, which was prevalent in government organizations at that time. Dr. Sreedharan had retired at the age of 58 as Member, Engineering from Railway Board in 1990 after which he took over as CMD of the Konkan Railway Project. As a compromise, Dr. Sreedharan was asked to assist in the selection of the Managing Director of the DMRC by the then Chief Minister of Delhi, Mr. Sahib Singh Verma, Lieutenant Governor, Mr. Tejendra khanna and Transport Minister of Delhi Mr. Rajendra Gupta. Though he came initially as a member of the search committee to find a Managing Director, the meeting ended with him being selected as the Managing Director. He, however, had a condition that he should be given a free hand to execute the project and to select people of his choice but the problem was how to appoint a person who was already 65 years of age. The matter went up to the highest level and a question was asked about his physical fitness at that age. A medical fitness test was conducted on Dr. Sreedharan by Railway doctors to overcome this hurdle and he was found fit. However, the recommendations concerning his age were creating obstacles but it was the then Cabinet Secretary Mr. T.S.R.Subramanium who overruled bureaucratic objections when he recorded on the file that when the Prime Minister of the country can govern the country at the age of 75, why can't Dr. Sreedharan be put in charge of this project. He recommended Dr. Sreedharan's appointment as Managing Director of DMRC which ultimately got the nod from the highest levels. It was rare to have a person of this age appointed. At that time when these papers were cleared it was already August 1997 and Dr. Sreedharan was at the fag end of finishing the Konkan Railway Project. He thus, was playing a dual role between August 1997 till November 1997 when he shuttled between Konkan Railway Corporation at Mumbai and the Delhi Metro Rail Corporation (DMRC) in Delhi. He had thus, informally already started looking after the affairs of the DMRC with the help of a few officers such as Mr. P.K.Gupta, Mr. D.D.Pahuja, Mrs. Saroj Rajwade and some of his colleagues from the Konkan Railway such as Mr. A.K.P.Unny, who was his OSD (Officer on special Duty) with an office in the Railway Board.

The DMRC in the early days thus, began from two rooms in the Ministry of Urban Development where Mr. Gupta, Mr. Pahuja and Mrs.Rajwade sat and from one room in Rail Bhawan in which Dr. Sreedharan and Mr. Unny operated. Dr. Sreedharan officially took over as Managing Director, DMRC on 4th Nov, 1997. At that time, the DMRC did not have an independent office but within one week the few others who had already joined DMRC alongwith the Managing Director shifted to NBCC Place located at Lodhi Road near Pragati Vihar Hostel which became the first proper office of the DMRC. Mr. Mangu Singh, the current MD of DMRC joined on 17 November 1997. The style of the working of this new organisation can be gauged from the fact that they were the first occupants of this building and decided to move in without electricity and water supply. It was from this office that the DMRC's plans were made and fructified. The office gradually expanded with the DMRC taking three floors of the building which coincided with the expansion of the organisation.

The first challenge faced by DMRC was finding the right personnel to build the Delhi Metro Project. The Delhi Metro was a rail based project and therefore the natural tendency was to gravitate towards rail based engineers and personnel specially since the Chief Executive also came from a Railway background. Railway engineers began to join in DMRC on deputation from December 1998 onwards. Inspite of them being from Railways, many of them didn't have exposure to Metro Rail systems, which are very different from normal Railway systems. Two teams were therefore, formed of about 20 engineers each covering diverse disciplines like civil engineering, electrical engineering and signaling and telecommunication engineering, which were sent on world tours covering 7-8 countries each to get an exposure of Metro technology and Metro systems internationally. Metro foreign tours were different from tours normally undertaken by government officers as the officers had very tight schedules during their travel abroad. At times, they only spent only 7-8 hours in one country before moving on to the next destination. The programmes were made in such a way that immediately on arrival at the airport, the Delhi Metro officers would leave for a meeting with foreign Metro rail officials or foreign Metro equipment manufacturers followed by a visit to their factory and the existing Metro rail lines in the city. There was almost no time for sightseeing or shopping which is normally associated with comfortable tours by officials.

An interesting aspect of the initial recruitment was the foresight of the Managing Director who had more than 40 years of service and he realised the need and importance for two crucial areas which are normally ignored by most organisations in India - Public Relations and the Legal branch. Both these areas could become stumbling blocks in the progress of the project. Dr. Sreedharan wanted the best people for these jobs but his handicap was that he was not an expert in these areas and so open advertisements were taken out to create heads of these departments who could build up these teams subsequently. In the case of Public Relations, the selection committee for the post of Chief Public Relations Officer consisted of an expert in this field who was brought in by him from Mumbai to evaluate the candidates. I was the selected applicant but I refused the job as I was reluctant to move from an established organisation like Indian Railways to a rather uncertain project with an uncertain future. However, a meeting with Dr. Sreedharan changed all this and I decided to join the Corporation on deputation after meeting with him. The track record of both the Public Relations and the Legal departments was crucial for the success of the Delhi Metro project. Projects can get badly derailed by stays granted by courts for years together. The DMRC emerged unscathed as the courts were very sympathetic and stays were not granted against the project. Court cases were carefully monitored, fought and information was supplied to the judiciary in detail by DMRC, which helped in deciding cases in favour of DMRC.

The DMRC scored on another front as their media handling throughout the duration of the project enabled it to establish itself as an organization which was efficient, transparent and fast. The DMRC received tremendous support from the newspapers and magazines who appreciated the functioning of this Corporation as they were regularly and timely briefed about all developments which took place in the Corporation. The media thus became a massive pillar of support to the Corporation though the DMRC did take some amount of flak from them during the aftermath of some accidents at the end of phase-II of the project.

On the media front, DMRC sold a dream to the common man of Delhi who was fed up of standing in long queues and sweating it out in packed DTC and Blueline buses. This was the first time that somebody had thought about the common man. More than 20,000 articles have already been published on Delhi Metro and over 90% of them have been positive.

Large-scale dissemination of information ensured that the public was well informed about the project at all stages and moved with the project through out. Advertising was not used as a means to inform the public thereby saving on cost and expenditure. This built up the DMRC brand name and reputation in the city and helped the DMRC in getting quick clearances for land acquisition, tree cutting, timely release of funds from the government, tax concession etc. as DMRC was projected as an organisation, which can perform, and the DMRC lived upto this reputation by building Phase-I of the project before time, within cost and without causing inconvenience to the public.

The way in which the original project was sanctioned initially would have led to the project probably becoming a failure since there would have been low ridership and low revenue as the routes were not along populated areas.

The first modification in the route of Delhi Metro was approved in August, 2000. Under this modification, the alignment of Line 1 of Phase- I was altered to include a heavily populated 15 kms stretch from Trinagar (now called Inderlok) to Barwala. This stretch replaced the earlier envisaged 19.3 kms Subzi Mandi- Holambi Kalan corridor of Phase-I, partly prompted by the lack of civic and commercial development along the earlier route. The corridor alteration was carried out to benefit innumerable homes, offices and industrial units of north-west Delhi. However, it was later decided to extend the Inderlok- Barwala line only up to Rithala as the three proposed stations after that (Daulatpur, Pehladpur and Barwala) had low population density.

In July 2002, the second modification in Phase-I was to include an 8.9 kms stretch from Barakhamba Road to Kirti Nagar and another 13.9 kms from Kirti Nagar to Dwarka as Line-3. The Barakhamba- Dwarka corridor replaced the proposed Trinagar (Inderlok)- Nangloi section. DMRC had earlier proposed to replace the Trinagar (Inderlok)- Nangloi line with a corridor linking Rajiv Chowk with Dilshad Garden via Vivek Vihar, Hargovind Enclave, Pratap Vihar and Vikas Marg. The proposal was, however, not sanctioned in the first phase by Delhi Government which decided on Barakhamba Road- Dwarka as the replacement corridor. A 6.5 kms extension into Dwarka sub city was also included in Phase-I later with DDA bearing the bulk of the cost at the initiative of Mr. Vijai Kapoor the then Lieutenant Governor of Delhi.

The DMRC management made dozens of presentations to ensure the above changes before the Government of Delhi and the Government of India on its own initiative as the impact would be tremendous for project success and for the people of Delhi. The original routes proposed on phase-I to Nangloi and Holambi Kalan would have resulted in the project becoming a white elephant and a disaster and the critics of the project would have ensured that no further lines would be sanctioned thus depriving the city residents of a much needed Mass Rapid Transit System (MRTS).

Another initiative of DMRC was to provide for an extra level below the existing Rajiv Chowk Metro station even though the line below (Dwarka line) had still not been sanctioned. In anticipation of the sanction, DMRC dug deeper without approval at Rajiv Chowk as it would not have been possible to do that later. Such type of engineering decisions involving money were boldly taken by DMRC which in most organizations would have been delayed as nobody wants to be saddled with problematic situations if the approval did not come later because, in such cases people feel it is better to be safe than to be sorry later.

Apart from these changes, DMRC went ahead at a fast pace with the planning of the first Metro section from Shahdara to Tis Hazari which was 8.3 kms long and was part of the originally approved corridor by the government and did not require any change.

It was a strategic move by the DMRC to begin work on this 8.3 kms immediately as this established the credibility of the DMRC as an organisation which can deliver the goods and displayed to the public that the project was actually happening on the ground. Detailed surveys took place, tenders were awarded and proceedings for land acquisition began in earnest. Tree cutting permissions were applied for and utilities were identified like water lines, sewer lines, telephone cables and electric lines, which would need to be diverted before the Metro construction could be taken up as the DMRC did not want to affect or disturb the life of the local people in the area, who would have been badly affected by disruption of electricity, water and communication connection to their houses. These disruptions would have upset the public and would have started generating a negative feeling about the Delhi Metro project and Metro construction, the same thing which happened when the Kolkata Metro Project was being constructed. Delhi Metro had to prove that they could construct the Metro in a different way.

To carry the public along with them, the Corporation began to organise Community Interaction Programmes at different localities through which the Metro would pass and construction activities would be carried out. These Community Interaction Programmes began as early as in the beginning of 1999 itself and acted as a safety valve in handling public grievances associated with large scale construction projects as any construction activity effects people of the area when it is undertaken, as roads need to be diverted, soil dug up and access had to be blocked for safety reasons in some of the localities. The DMRC decided to inform the public about these inconveniences by openly coming out infront of them. The Resident's Welfare Associations and local public were called and special meetings were organised at a fixed date and time by the DMRC in which representatives from Public Relations and the Chief Engineer concerned were present. If required, other officers from the Police, Jal Board, Delhi Government etc. were also called depending upon the type of questions expected at these meetings. The meetings were normally held in a community hall at the affected locality itself so that the residents could easily attend these meetings and were informed about them. Politicians were not separately invited for these meetings but could attend as these were open forums for the public. The DMRC directly interacted with the public on issues related with their construction and were able to redress the grievances of the public face to face directly, thus, eliminating outside interference on small issues during the construction of the Metro in the city. People normally had small problems such as access to their houses, disruption of utility services, and construction of small boundary walls etc. which were major issues for them in their daily lives but could easily be resolved by any large construction organisation at hardly any cost. Even if we could not solve all their problems, the mere fact that here was an organisation which was openly willing to come to the public and listen to them in their area was greatly appreciated by the public of Delhi. The Bhagidari concept adopted by Delhi Government subsequently, is based upon the same pattern with one difference. In the Bhagidari scheme of things, the RWAs have to come to a central location in the city to meet the officers, whereas, the DMRC used to go to the colonies directly to interact with the public. Hundreds of such Community Interaction Programmes were organised in areas such as Rohini, Shahdara, Dilshad Garden, GTB Nagar, Tilak Nagar, Karkarduma, Nirman Vihar, Mall Road etc. Many such interactions were held on holidays as only those days suited the local residents who were not available on normal working days. However, many suggestions were received to change the alignment, which Metro officials could not agree to since these were larger issues to be decided by the Government and changing the alignment or changing the requirement for land was a sensitive issue.

The decision to have foreign consultants

After DMRC's basic organizational structure was in place, it decided to establish its own technical capabilities in order to ensure that the Metro network was upto international standards. In order to achieve this, DMRC called for tenders for appointment of General Consultants. While the bidding started out with the submission of six tenders, soon the bidders had formed into three consortia for which DMRC evaluated technical and financial bids. It then entered into negotiations with the consortium that had the highest ranked bid (comprising Pacific Consultants International (PCI), Parsons Brinkerhoff International (PBI), Japan Railway Technical Service (JARTS), Tonichi Engineering Consultants and Rail India Technical and Economical Services (RITES). Although the cost of the contract was estimated at close to ₹ 4 billion, the final contract was awarded at ₹ 2 billion as the man-month requirement was brought down from ₹ 14,000 to ₹ 8,000 during negotiations and a provisional letter of acceptance was issued in June 1998 to the selected agency. PCI were also the in-house consultants for the Japan Bank of International Cooperation (JBIC) and this led to speculation in the media about whether the appointment had been completely open and transparent. So intense was the scrutiny that the government took up the matter for an in – depth examination. The DMRC stood by its decision and openly disclosed details when called upon to clarify the process of bidding and appointment on several occasions. The government finally cleared the selection process and a newspaper that had printed incorrect information on the bidding process, issued a public apology.

Battle of the Gauges

Many important technical decisions needed to be taken before construction on the Metro lines could begin and one of the most crucial was whether DMRC should use broad gauge or standard gauge for the Metro in Delhi. In 1999, almost 90% of Metro networks across the world used standard gauge. Not only was the standard gauge the choice for Metro systems in most developed nations, it also provided better speed, maneuverability and safety, while also allowing for sharper and therefore space saving turns on the tracks. However, the Ministry of Railways (Railway Board) was in favour of adopting the broad gauge, which it felt would facilitate inter-connectivity of rolling stock between the Rail and Metro networks and was in keeping with the 'unigauge' policy for India. The Delhi Metro did not agree that inter – running of trains between the Metro and railway tracks was feasible. After discussions and debates spanning a year and a half, the situation reached a point where Dr. Sreedharan could either, continue to lock horns with the Ministry of Railways and risk further delay, or concede to the Ministry's demand. Dr. Sreedharan chose the latter course of action though on the night of August 4, 2000, When the Group of Ministers (GOM) declared the final decision to use broad gauge, he was tempted to resign but was dissuaded from doing so by Mr. Vijai kapoor the Lieutenant Governer of Delhi. Over time, Dr. Sreedharan was able to persuade the ministry to reverse its stand and use standard gauge for the upcoming Metro lines. Almost 61.4 kilometers of Phase II tracks used Standard Gauge and the entire Phase-III network of the DMRC is being planned on standard gauge. Unfortunately, due to the use of different gauges, interchangeability of stock within the two phases of the Metro continues to remain a problem.

All new Metros coming up in the country now are also on standard gauge keeping in view the International practice and advantages.

Technology

The Delhi Metro was being built from 1998 onwards, therefore, the company had an option of either going in for a old and conventional Metro System or on the other hand they could adopt the latest technical features from the new Metros such as Singapore and Hongkong. The DMRC decided to take advantage of the fact that they came into the field of Metro technology very late and thus, took a decision to adopt extremely modern air conditioned rolling stock with Automatic Train Protection and Automatic Train operations system rather than going in for conventional suburban trains. Terrestrial Trunk Radio (TETRA) was adopted to ensure trouble free communication and DMRC became the first Metro to adopt 25 kV rigid Over Head electrical (OHE) systems for an underground Metro . A paperless ticketless system was adopted with the AFC system of DMRC being the most advanced since they were the first Metro to have contactless tokens for single journeys. It was decided that the Delhi Metro should run on advanced ballast less tracks thus, minimising the need for track maintenance and long welded rails ensuring that track joints are minimised thus, providing more riding comfort and reduced noise levels.

The Legal Framework

As DMRC was ready to start operating the Metro on a day–to–day basis, they found to their surprise that a legal cover for the project was not there. This left the entire project exposed to all types of legal issues and potential litigation – something that could not only slow progress on the construction of the remaining lines but which would also make operations of the Metro Rail system difficult. As the Prime Minister of India was set to inaugurate the Metro line on a fixed date i.e. December 24, 2002, an ordinance was promulgated two months before the inauguration, and subsequently the Delhi Metro Operations and Maintenance Act was passed during the next session of the Parliament. This Act listed the powers of the Metro administration (such as acquiring land and entering into contracts) and provided for, among various other things the constitution of a Fare Fixation Committee and the appointment of a Commissioner of Metro Railway Safety. The Fare Fixation Committee ensured that Metro fares would be fixed on realistic lines as the committee was headed by a High Court Judge and would not be decided on populistic requirements. The Commissioner for Metro Railway Safety was necessary as without safety clearance, the Metro system could not be made operational and open for public use.

Financial Concessions

Though DMRC had requested for import and excise duty concessions for the equipment and rolling stock imported by the organisation, neither the Government of India nor the Government of Delhi provided any tax exemption to it during the initial stages of the project. However, once the first train was ready to be launched ahead of time and the Government of India was convinced that DMRC would be able to deliver the Metro on time, it agreed to grant the Delhi Metro project customs and excise duty concessions amounting to ₹ 14.07 billion in 2002. In addition, the Government of Delhi waived sales tax and works contract tax to the extent of ₹ 3.93 billion . Both the Centre and State Governments provided several other tax concessions as the project progressed in Phase-I and in Phase-II also

Underground Issues

Almost 20 percent covering 13.17 kilometers of Phase I was built entirely underground. At Chawri Bazar, the entire station was built inside an underground tunnel at a depth of 25 meters. While digging around the Nayi Sadak area in old Delhi for the line connecting Delhi Main to Chawri Bazaar, initially the construction contractors used the Tunnel Boring Method (TBM). However, the digging faced several delays, as the cutter head of the Tunnel Boring Machine could not cut through the rocks and broke. After extending the contractor's deadline by several months and bringing in an extra machine, progress remained limited due to the hard and abrasive nature of the rocks in that area. Finally, with DMRC pushing for it, the contractors switched to the New Austrian Tunneling Method from the opposite end in order to complete the tunneling within the allocated deadline. The construction team had to reconfigure the entire approach while dealing with several challenges like water seepage within the tunnel. Had DMRC waited to renegotiate the construction contracts, it may not have been able to operationalize the line within the allocated time of two years. Instead, DMRC used its existing goodwill and fast decision making process to convince the contractors to proceed along the new approach and completed the section by the target date. This was accomplished without disturbing the over ground historical surface of the Chawri Bazaar area which had many old structures from the Mughal era.

Difficulty in Getting Land

Project Affected Persons (PAPs) or people who would be affected due to the proposed alignment of the Metro routes protested against some of the planned routes demanding realignment. One of the controversial areas was the Metro line near an area where a large section of the legal fraternity had their offices near Kashmere Gate/Tis Hazari. As they were not happy with the fact that they would have to relocate to alternate office spaces, a group of lawyers asked for a meeting to discuss the issue with the Chief Minister of Delhi, Smt. Sheila Dikshit who supported the DMRC, stating that experts proficient at their job had planned the alignment, and while she would do, everything in her power to help those inconvenienced, realignment was out of the question. The DMRC subsequently dealt with a number of such alignment issues and minimized disruption to the daily lives of people living in nearby areas, without altering their technical plans.

They used a similar approach while dealing with land acquisition issues. As per the laws, the government could easily acquire private land needed for development projects by suitably compensating the landowner. However, by making personal visits and engaging with landowners, the DMRC ensured that land was handed over to the organisation without too many problems. The Metro alignment was fixed in such a way that the need for private land acquisition was kept to the minimum. The personal attention paid to the issue by Mr. C.B.K. Rao, the then Director (Projects) helped curb any mutinous tendencies, thereby avoiding costly and time-consuming litigation in a number of cases.

The shifting of religious structures is a ticklish and sensitive issue . A number of small temples were encountered near the Metro alignment at many places. All these were relocated by holding direct discussions by DMRC engineers with the temple priests with the understanding that the original temples would be shifted brick by brick to the new locations by the Metro construction engineers. In one case near Shahdara a new idol was procured all the way from Jaipur spending extra money which was transported to Delhi and placed in the newly relocated temple. In a particular instance, the government needed to rehabilitate approximately 300 shopkeepers near Shahdra before DMRC could use the land. Instead of waiting for the relevant government departments to work out how and where they would resettle the shopkeepers, DMRC engaged in discussions with the affected persons and with their concurrence, bought land close by where they constructed shops and provided this to the displaced traders for a nominal price.

Metro- A Mission

In 1997, one of the first things that the DMRC did was to have a Corporate Mission and Corporate Culture so that the whole organization could work towards a specific goal. The Corporate Mission was as below:

Corporate Mission

1. To make the first phase of the Delhi MRTS fully operational by March 2005.
2. To complete the Project within the estimated cost.
3. To make it a world class Metro; a vehicle to promote dignity and discipline in the city.

After Phase- I of the Delhi Metro was completed, the organization immediately modified its Corporate Mission keeping in view the new requirements of DMRC and today it reads as under:-

Corporate Mission

1. To cover whole of Delhi with a Metro network by the year 2021.
2. Delhi Metro to be of world class standards in regard to safety, reliability, punctuality, comfort and customer satisfaction.
3. Metro to operate on sound commercial lines obviating the need for Government support.

The DMRC also defines its Corporate Culture which is as below:

Corporate Culture

1. We should be totally dedicated and committed to the Corporate Mission.
2. Personal integrity should never be in doubt – we should maintain full transparency in all our decisions and transactions.

3. The Organization must be lean but effective.
4. Corporation must project an image of efficiency, transparency, courtesy and "we mean business" attitude.
5. Our construction activities should not inconvenience or endanger public life nor should lead to ecological or environmental degradation.
6. All our structures should be aesthetically planned and well maintained.
7. Safety of Metro user is our paramount responsibility.
8. Our stations and trains should be spotlessly clean.
9. Staff should be smartly dressed, punctual, polite and helpful to the customers.
10. Employees should discharge their responsibilities with pride, perfection and dignity.

The above communication is there on all the official files of the DMRC and is displayed prominently in the Metro Training School, Metro New Year Dairy and other places to reinforce these values among Metro employees.

DMRC Management

Case studies on the Delhi Metro Rail Corporation's management style have been developed by the Harvard Business School, USA and the Indian Institute of Management, Ahmedabad in India

The management style in DMRC is unique and is not based upon any textbook knowledge garnered from any management institute. It is based upon practical experience and the salient features of the same are as below:-

1. Head of Departments (HoDs) Meeting: There is a meeting held on every Monday morning at 9:30 AM sharp that is attended by the Managing Director (MD), all full-time Directors and all HoDs of DMRC. There are, thus, about 50 such top managers who attend this meeting every week.

   In this meeting, weekly targets are set and issues discussed in the previous meeting are reviewed to check how far they have been implemented successfully. There are no written minutes of this meeting and this meeting helps all the HoDs to work as a team as each one comes to know what the other department is doing and what are the common organizational goals for which the team has to function.

   Once every month, the officers who are of the middle management i.e, Deputy Chief Engineers (Dy. CEs), DGM and above are also invited to attend the HoD meeting so that there is vertical communication within the organization also. This helps the middle management in becoming aware about the management philosophy and needs and also helps in percolation of information and direction at different levels. In addition, this also gives an opportunity for the middle management to speak to the top management on any issue which may be bothering them or their staff below. This also acts as an important feedback tool.

2. Spiritualism: The DMRC distributes a copy of the 'Bhagavad Gita' to all its officers and very small snippets picked up from varied spiritual texts are sometimes used to motivate the employees to perform better.

3. Decision making in DMRC is very fast and it is possible to get a decision on an issue on the same day from the highest levels of management within the organization. The decisions are clear-cut and are not ambiguous. They are not postponed for a later date. Clear-cut 'YES' or 'NO' instructions are issued on every issue.

The tendency to pass the buck or delay is not at all encouraged and often results in castigation of the offender. Target orientation and quick implementation is the guiding force in decision making keeping in view the best interests of the organization in mind. Even if a wrong decision is taken, it is condoned provided the management feels that there is no mal-intentation while taking the decision which has been done in good faith.

4. The DMRC management follows all the rules and regulations adopted by the government and all records are maintained properly. The movement of papers in DMRC is much faster and decision making is very quick. Audit and Vigilance systems as practiced in Public Sector Units (PSUs) in India exist and are active within the organization.

5. The unique structuring of the DMRC is another interesting aspect of the management as this company is owned 50% by the Government of Delhi and 50% by the Government of India which are the equity contributors to the project. The corporation, therefore, is represented by the nominees of Central and the State Government in equal measure and there were times when different political parties were holding sway at the Centre and in the State. Inspite of this, the DMRC management remained completely professional and focused on the construction of the Metro Project and was non-aligned with any party. Thus, Smt. Sheila Dikshit, the Chief Minister of Delhi had described the Delhi Metro as an example of political parties following different ideologies coming together on the issue of development while Mr. Atal Bihari Vajpayee, the then Prime Minister of India said "..Everybody has cooperated for the Metro. How can there not be cooperation between Delhi's Bharat Sarkar (Central Government) and Delhi's Delhi Sarkar (State Government)?" . Mr. L.K.Advani who was the Deputy Prime Minister of India earlier had also said "The success of Metro is due to the synergy between Japanese Government and Indian Government, the synergy between the Centre and State Government and the synergy between technocrats and politicians" .

गन्तव्य स्थान \Destina
DMRC
MBA Stu
Universit

elcomes
dents from
of Minnesota

The uniqueness of the management style of DMRC is a subject of interest for management schools in India and abroad. Students from management institutions have been coming regularly to the DMRC since 2003 to understand the methods adopted by the DMRC to ensure that the Delhi Metro Project was completed within schedule and cost inspite of the difficult environment. Among the colleges who have come for this purpose are:

Yale School of Management, USA, Stanford Graduate School of Business, USA, Carlson School of Management, University of Minnesota, Columbia Business School, Columbia University, New York, Dallas Baptist University, USA, Universite de Rouen, France Darden School of Business, University of Virginia, USA, Sanjose University, USA, Philadelphia University, USA, Wharton School, University of Pennsylvania, Rotman School of Management, University of Toronto, Utrecht University, Netherlands DeSales University, Pennsylvania, USA , Harvard University's Kennedy School of Government, University of Pennsylvania, USA, Twente University (Netherlands) London University, UK, etc.

Some interesting opinions expressed on the functioning of the Delhi Metro by former Presidents, Prime Ministers about the management style of the Delhi Metro Rail Corporation include:

The Prime Minister of India Dr. Manmohan Singh in December 2004 said that he was truly impressed by the quality of the new infrastructure built by DMRC and felt that the organization had set an example for all Indians to follow howsoever difficult the task. He said that the attitude of the DMRC should inspire all of us rather than the 'chalta hai' attitude. The Hon'ble Prime Minister travelled on the Delhi Metro and said that "I do think we now have a service that can compete with the best in the world."

Integrity

As the lamp in a windless place does not flicker – that is thought to be the comparison of the Yogi of controlled mind practising union with self through Dhaynayoga.

Verse 19 of Chapter 6 of the Bhagavad Gita published in 'Metro News' Volume 88

DOGRA

Nirula's

Integrity in DMRC is perceived as not only being honest but is considered as a wider concept in which others perceive you to be honest. This means that just being personally honest is not enough but people around you should feel that you are an honest person.

All officers who are in the executive cadre in DMRC are given a copy of the Bhagavad Gita called Gita Makaranda which has been written by Swami Vidyaprakashananda of Sri Suka Brahma Ashram of Sri Kalahasti in Chittoor District of Andhra Pradesh. This copy was picked up out of all the versions of Gita which are available in India after I had once asked Dr. Sreedharan, which is the version of the Gita, that one should read since there are so many varieties and versions available which causes confusion. He gave me this version and indeed I found it an excellent reading as each stanza of the Gita is very well explained for the lay reader, who is being initiated into spiritualism. Subsequently, a copy of this Gita was procured for every executive of DMRC and today all Metro officers receive a copy on their joining the organization.

The Bhagavad Gita is treated by the DMRC as a management manual and not as a spiritual or religious text as it explains how a person should manage himself so that he can function efficiently and can give his maximum output in every situation. This is exemplified in the Gita when a completely demoralized and de-motivated warrior Arjun is motivated to perform excellently by Lord Sri Krishna and the text of this message is given in the Bhagavad Gita.

In the DMRC, all employees are required to sign a code of ethics whose main contents are : -

- DMRC employees should work with professionalism, honesty and integrity
- No employees shall indulge in giving or taking any illegal gratification, monitary or otherwise
- No employee shall indulge in lobbying for/or propose any honour or reward/ award for himself
- No employee shall use his official position to further his personal interest
- No employee shall indulge in any trade or side business in his name
- No employee shall indulge in collection of any donation for any cause whatsoever without the management's prior approval

- No employee shall indulge in socially inappropriate behavior like indulging in bigamy, extra marital alliance etc.
- Every employee shall assist and cooperate with the government to eliminate bribery, fraud or corruption.
- Every employee shall spend every single rupee in the official discharge of his duty with diligence

In many of the Monday meetings of the top managers of DMRC (Heads of Departments Meetings), some shlokas from spiritual leaders are used and discussed to motivate the top managers.

Special competency building workshops are also being organized by the Human Resource department of DMRC in which employees are given management talks for inculcating good values such as morality, integrity, punctuality, diligence, hard work etc.

This emphasis on integrity has definitely helped the organization as it helps in getting the human mind to think because as per the law of karma you have to pay for your actions in this life or the next life. As such reading the Gita gets your mind thinking that if you are dishonest you will have to pay for it in some way or the other. As such even if a person does something wrong, he has this in the back of his mind that someday he may have to pay for it in his balance sheet of good and bad deeds. This mental triggering helps in inculcating values such as honesty and thereby helps in curbing the levels of corruption which otherwise may flow freely in any organization since unfortunately, these values have not been reinforced by our educational system at the school level.

The level of commitment of DMRC Officers in the initial stage was so high that at times people reported for duty within two days of suffering an extreme bereavement such as the loss of a life partner or a parent to ensure that the work was done on time.

Professional Competency

State of the art Shastri Park Training School provides training in all spheres of Metro technology to ensure professional competency among its employees.

Every person has to be professionally competent in his field of activity. Therefore, an engineer working in the DMRC was expected to be fully qualified for his job with enough experience in the field to undertake the job allotted to him. In case, some training was required to increase the competency, the same was imparted by DMRC by sending the engineers for specialized training programmes which included visits to international rail systems such as Singapore, Hong kong, Japan, Taipei etc. to increase their professional exposure to the work culture and techniques adopted by foreign engineers. The DMRC was thus able to harness an extremely competent team of civil, electrical, signalling and telecommunications engineers.

Some Metro engineers were also attached to the foreign consultancy group giving advise to DMRC called General Consultants - Pacific Consultants, Parsons Brikenhoff, Japan Railway Technical Service, Rail India Technical & Eco Services on a full time basis so that they could absorb technical knowledge from these foreign consultants directly. The engineers were attached for a period ranging from three to five months and subsequently they came back to DMRC bringing with them the necessary technical know how. Today, the DMRC engineers are self sufficient in many areas such as civil engineering and almost all civil construction works are carried out indigenously. In other areas also, the Delhi Metro engineers are now able to match knowledge levels with the best available in Europe and the United States.

The selection to the DMRC initially was largely from the Indian Railways since Metro was essentially a Rail based technology. Subsequently; people from other departments joined the organization at the middle and top levels.

At the initial and basic levels of entry, recruitment was started since the beginning of the project through an all India competitive exam which consisted of a written test, interview and a detailed medical examination on the patterns followed by the Union Public Service Commission (UPSC) and the Staff Selection Commission (SSC) of the Government of India. This was done deliberately to eliminate entry of people into DMRC through pulls, pressures and influences, as the tendency is to consider Public Sector Units as a convenient recruitment ground for favourites. Such people putting pressures were firmly told that all recruitment is done through open selection which is advertised in newspapers based upon merit. This enabled the DMRC to recruit people of good calibre and quality rather than being burdened with unnecessary and incompetent people who would have been thrust upon the organization. The DMRC has thus, evolved into a professionally manned company.

In the initial stages in 1998, groups of Metro officers were sent to visit different Metros so that they could gather the experience and exposure of International Metros since many of these officers had never seen any Metro apart from Kolkata Metro. Twenty officers were clubbed together into one group and were sent to South East Asia and Japan while another similar group was sent to Europe for about twenty days. This brought all the officers onto a certain mental wavelength about the competency and technical calibre subsequently expected from them during the implementation of the Delhi Metro Project. Though this accounted for a cost of almost 4 lakhs per person to the DMRC, It was money well spent.

The DMRC established its own training school in the beginning of 2002 at Shastri Park to train the young boys and girls who would take up frontline positions such as train operators, station controllers, junior engineers etc. This training school was the first of its kind where the trainers were trained at Hongkong where they underwent 3-4 months training programmes since such facilities were not available in India. The group of trainers then started imparting training to the new recruits based upon what they had learnt from Hongkong Metro. Most of these trainers were Indian Railway employees who had joined the DMRC on deputation. Today, this training school is the only one of its kind in South Asia with its own auditorium, specialized classrooms, simulators and practical training laboratories and is also imparting training to other new Metros coming up in India.

Every morning all Metro trainees are required to say a prayer which is sung by them in the presence of faculty members. The prayer reads:

> Itni Shakti Hame De Na Daataa
> Manka Vishvaas Kamazor Ho Naa
> Hum Chale Nek Raaste Pe Humse
> Bhulkar Bhii Koi Bhul Ho Naa...

This prayer has been taken from the movie 'Ankush' and was picked up by a young Metro official who was the first Principal of this school. It basically inspires, motivates and enthuses you to perform well as singing the song creates a positive mental framework to the individual to face the challenges of the day well.

How Metro overcame the Murphy's Law?

On 24th December 2002, when the Prime Minister of India was to open the first section, DMRC had only one substation at Kashmere Gate feeding 220 kV. While highly unlikely, there was still an apparent risk of system failure. Many other organizations might have overlooked such a risk but DMRC was committed to displaying its quality and insisted on a backup, but there was no other alternative available.

However, the concerned DMRC official noticed that the Northern Railways have an independent supply at Dadri and a substation at Sahibabad. DMRC requested them for help and laid one line till Shahdara (25 kV) as a backup arrangement, at extra costs.

On 24th December, the Prime Minister was the first citizen to ride on the Metro. The journey started at 10.10 am and then at 10.20 the power supply was disrupted. Within a minute the backup system took over without anyone even noticing the failure of the primary system.

On the day of the inauguration of the Metro, with the who's who of Indian politics on board, and with the media watching every move, Murphy's Law held itself, since careful preparation and commitment had been put in place to go the extra mile, and the embarrassment was avoided.

"Satish Kumar, Director (Electrical)/DMRC during interaction with the Indian Institute of Management- Ahmedabad"

It takes two to three years to build an elevated Metro station normally. The DMRC had to build one elevated station in only eight months at Chhattarpur since the land could be acquired only eight months before the target date for opening the line due to prolonged litigation. They still built the station on time by innovative engineering and advance planning – The station was prefabricated in steel in advance separately and only assembled at the site in eight months to meet the target.

HEAD LIGHT
PARKING BRAKE OFF

SIEMENS
POWER FAULT
AUXILIARY FAULT
VCB TRIP
EMERGENCY BRAKE
PARKING BRAKE
SPARE

Metro Symbols

To establish and reinforce togetherness and camaraderie within the organization and to establish a separate brand image for DMRC employees and DMRC as a distinct organization, the following Metro symbols were developed:

Logo

Mascot

MD's Award Medals

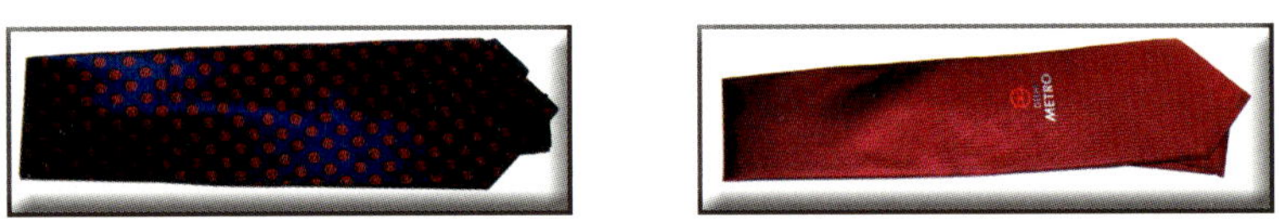

Ceremonial Ties

Target Orientation

Reverse countdown clocks ensured timely completion of projects within the set deadlines.

ANTONOV
DESIGN BUREAU
INTERNATIONAL CARGO
TRANSPORTER
Phone:+38(044)454-28-60
Fax:+38(044)454-28-52
E-mail: sales@antonov.kiev.ua
BOMBARDIER
BOMBARDIER

ONAL CARGO
RANSPORTER
Phone:+38(044)454-28-60
Fax:+38(044)454-28-32
E-mail: sales@antonov.kiev.ua
ANTONOV 124-100M-150

The philosophy in DMRC has been that the projects are set targets, depending upon the time available and the work is planned and executed in such a way that the final target is met even before the scheduled time. Generally, if a person is given 10 days to complete a job, he will do it in the same time with most of the work being done in the last 2 or 3 days. While the government gave 10 years to DMRC to build Phase – I, DMRC set much tighter internal targets which ensured the completion of the work in only 7 years and 3 months. Human psychology is such that we all tend to relax in the initial stages and start rushing only towards the end. If we recollect our own exam days, most students start studying only a few days before the exams and are found reading till the last minute.

The Metro thus set tight internal targets for all its lines which were monitored very carefully at all times. In Phase -I, there were three lines and each had a target which was watched through a reverse 'countdown clock' which used to show the number of days left for completion of each line. Thus if 400 days were left in line X today then tomorrow the reverse 'countdown clock' would show that only 399 days are left to complete line X. This, therefore, was a psychological management technique aimed at constantly reminding all employees about the time left for target implementation for each section.

In phase II, the DMRC constructed 125 kms in only 4 ½ years – a feat which has never been achieved in any democratic society keeping in view the difficulties in getting legal, official and other sanctions related to project implementation. In contrast, the implementation of the Kolkata Metro Project took almost 25 years to complete only one line of approximately 16 kms length.

Time saved is money saved and DMRC calculated that, for every day that the project was delayed would cost the DMRC ₹ 2.3 crores extra per day in inflationary cost and loss of operational revenue in Phase I. In Phase II, each day's delay would have resulted in an additional cost of ₹ 4.3 crores per day loss approximately. This fact was drilled into all Metro employees so that they realized the importance of time in project implementation. Each day was important.

People working on the project thus normally never ever thought about going on leave for long spells. In my own fourteen years with the DMRC I have never taken more than a few days leave and that too in emergencies.

Metro Train coaches were airlifted by special Antonov Aircraft and brought to Delhi to save time in Phase-II as the sea route would have taken longer.

Role of Finance

Availibility of enough funds and timely payments to all contractors kept the project moving non stop.

The Finance department in the DMRC has played a very important role and is considered a part of the Executive. The Finance officers attend all the technical meetings so that they are fully briefed about the developments and requirements of the executives and time is not wasted in unnecessary cross notings on the files between the Finance department and the Executive. The Finance department, thus has full knowledge about the need and justification for items.

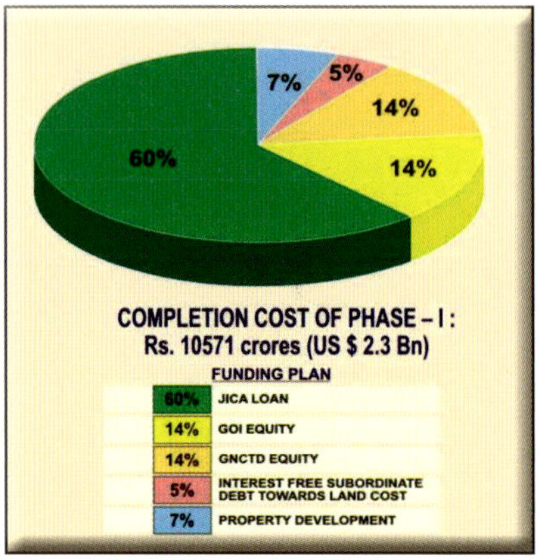

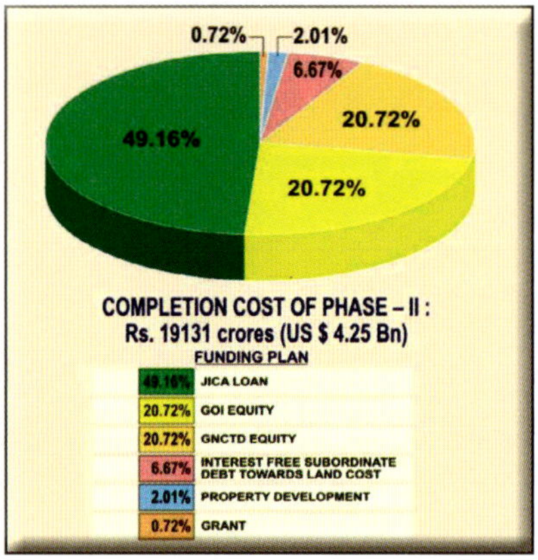

The Metro philosophy also viewed the contractors as DMRC's partners and keeping this sprit in mind, the Finance department of Delhi Metro ensured timely payments of all dues to the contractors. The moment the contractor's bill was received, the payments were released in three to four days and in case a certain portion of the bill was disputed, only the disputed amount was held back and the rest of the amount was released immediately without delay. Even the disputed amount was required to be sorted out within a week's time and payments were released to the contractors.

No contractor puts in money from his pocket and a contractor will work only if you pay him. Therefore, it is essential to pay the contractors on time if you want to ensure timely completion of the project. Delay in payments also leads to corruption, therefore, every contractor has always been asked by the top Management repeatedly whether they are facing any problem from DMRC with regard to payments.

All payments realized are displayed electronically so that the contractors know the position of their pending payments online.

> *The tough side of the Finance department was visible in the Central Secretariat-Badarpur Line when Bank Guarantees of non performing contractors was encashed.*
>
> *R.N.Joshi, Director (Finance)*

Role of Legal Department

Legal Department helped DMRC in avoiding court stays and removing unnecessary bottlenecks in the way.

Pratibha Industries Limited

The Metro management recognized the need to have a very strong Legal department, if they were going to be able to execute the project on time. Therefore, a full fledged Legal department was set up from the beginning itself, since the DMRC realized that there would be lots of litigation on issues such as land acquisition, property taxation, excise and custom duties, labour laws, personnel matters, contractual disputes, arbitration etc.

All these disputes needed to be very well defended legally at all stages from the lower courts upto the Supreme Court. The Legal department was able to gather all the points from the concerned user departments of DMRC and was able to present effective counter arguments at each stage of the litigation before all the courts. Usually, the head of the Legal department himself was present in the court at all sensitive hearings along with the chief engineer or concerned head of the department who was dealing with the subject, which was coming up for hearing. The Managing Director of DMRC himself took a lot of interest in all court cases as he realized the sensitivity of the issues, since adverse judgments would not only delay the project but would have huge financial implications. The Metro's track record in court cases was excellent and they were able to win most of the cases. Very few stays were granted against the project as the judiciary also understood the need to have a Mass Transit System for the benefit of the public of Delhi.

The Metro management had issued instructions to all head of the departments to provide full cooperation by giving complete facts of all cases to the Legal department, well in time so that they could prepare arguments for defence properly. It was thus, mandatory for all heads of the departments to personally attend court hearings to ensure that proper information was given in the court in case of any cross questioning. Each case was monitored by the management carefully.

This approach of treating the Legal department as a frontline department has helped in project execution as many organizations, tend to give routine weightage to such issues. DMRC was thus able to get quick and fast decisions from the judiciary by constantly monitoring and arguing cases properly in the courts.

In arbitration cases also, the DMRC has had a good track record with it being able to defend their position very well against the contractors when the claims were raised.

₹100 cr per annum is saved by DMRC for property tax with the High Court's judgment classifying Metro as a Railway.

DELHI METRO

Role of Public Relations

More than 20, 000 positive news articles and stories generated by the Public Relations Department helped DMRC in establishing itself as a 'brand' in the market.

The management of the Delhi Metro realized the need to have a professional Public Relations set up, if they were going to successfully implement such a huge urban infrastructure construction project, especially since this was being done in the capital city of India which has more than 200 television and radio channels, newspapers, magazines, websites etc. which are actively watching all events which takes place in Delhi. Thus, even the smallest incident in Delhi gets massive coverage at the local and at times national and international levels, since the camera teams and reporters are readily available close by in this VIP city. In contrast, if the construction had been taking place in a rural area or a small town, the construction agency could get away with a few mistakes as the media is not present constantly at those locations. In Delhi however, the Delhi Metro Project required a very effective Public Relations team to handle regular dissemination of information to the media and since 1998 almost 20,000 articles and news items on the Delhi Metro Project have been published, most of which are positive. Infact, the entire DMRC brand image has been built up through effective Public Relations, without resorting to expensive advertising.

Media Relations was the main focus of Public Relations with one to one interaction with reporters who were regularly briefed on all developments on the project. They were constantly taken for site visits so that they could get a feel of the project and would appreciate the difficulties and challenges faced during the construction. The main focus was on print media and electronic media was constantly regulated keeping in view security and other concerns. It is very important to effectively control the media in successful project implementation as bad newspaper reporting can be very dangerous for an organization as these reports are read by the public, the politicians and the bureaucrats. Negative reporting and fault finding would have resulted in enquiry commissions being set up and interference in project implementation. Careful media handling resulted in extremely good stories of the project, which helped in developing a positive public tone and image of DMRC which was further reflected in the complete freedom and non interference given to the top management of DMRC during project implementation.

Other media tools which were used were very limited, like use of exhibitions with mock up wooden train models displayed at the India International Trade Fair (IITF) between 1998 and 2002 before the actual Metro train came to Delhi, and other innovative low cost ideas such as Nukkad Nataks (Street Plays) to educate the local public in socio-economically backward areas. Where ever the Metro was being constructed, these tools helped DMRC in establishing a good rapport with the local public. The entire DMRC Brand has been built with almost zero spending on advertising with complete concentration on timely and regular dissemination of information to the media.

A special study on the PR strategy adopted by DMRC was commissioned by the JICA (Japan International Cooperation Agency) in 2005 so that the DMRC example could be emulated in other projects funded by the Japanese Government.

Officials

Officers were selected solely on the basis of their professional competence, integrity and efficiency that helped DMRC in achieving excellence.

Delicate handling of officials is essential if one has to successfully implement a project in India. This is because of the inherent nature of the system in our country where powers and controls are in their hands. In DMRC, there is a Board of Directors consisting of 16 Directors out of which 6 are in-house Directors while the rest are Senior Officers representing the Government of Delhi and the Goverment of India (Ministry of Urban Development) who are the equity owners of the Delhi Metro Project. Overall, the Board of Directors have supported and fully backed the recommendations of the organisation.

An advantage which DMRC has enjoyed is that all executive powers were given to the Managing Director who could decide the tenders irrespective of their values. He only had to keep the Board apprised about the tenders beyond a certain value. The MD had full powers with regard to agreements/appointments within the DMRC and as a result of these wide sweeping powers, very quick decisions could be taken by the DMRC which did not have to seek approvals and sanctions from the Government in finalizing tenders on day to day matters.

However, there were tussles in the initial stages regarding awarding of tenders but the DMRC held firm and did not budge from its stand. This naturally resulted in the development of resentment against the Metro management within some sections but since the organisation continued to perform in an excellent manner and completed its target within budget and before time, there was no interference. The personal stature of the Managing Director, Dr. Elattuvalapil Sreedharan, who himself was a retired Secretary of the Government of India (Retired as Member, Engineering, Railway Board) and came with a big reputation of integrity, honesty and professional competence, since he had already executed the difficult Konkan Railway Project after his retirement from Indian Railways, helped in controlling external forces within and outside to a great extent.

Many officers who joined the DMRC on deputation came from government organizations and were of the level of deputy secretary (Junior administrative grade) and joint secretary (Senior administrative grade) & could, therefore, interact with their batch mates in the Delhi Government and Central Government on equal terms. Initially, when the DMRC started, it took some time for government officers to understand that the Metro officers were slightly different from regular public sector undertaking officers. This definitely helped in getting faster clearances from the government agencies.

For an organisation which was performing well, the Government also provided institutional backing through a High Powered Committee headed by the Chief Secretary, Delhi and an Empowered Committee headed by the Cabinet Secretary which helped in sorting out DMRC's inter-departmental and problematic issues expeditiously.

On 3rd May, 2009 during the Foundation Day celebration of DMRC, the Lieutenant Governor of Delhi Mr. Tejendra Khanna described the DMRC as a 24 carat gold standard organization as it has completed projects ahead of time. He said that the Delhi Metro is a shining example of what can be achieved by dedicated professionals combining high ethical integrity with excellent domain knowledge, commitment to quality and sustained, disciplined hard work .

Punctuality

Punctuality of over 99% in Metro train operations is maintained on all days and if a train is late by even 60 seconds, it is considered to have lost punctuality in Delhi Metro

06:34

In the Delhi Metro punctuality is sacrosanct as punctuality is a courtesy to the person and persons with whom you are going to interact since his time or their time is as precious and valuable as your own. Coming even a minute late is considered impolite and inappropriate. This was drilled into all DMRC officers and staff from the first day. Therefore, arrival at office at 9 am which was the time of the opening of the office was considered absolutely essential as it was felt that if you are late for office you will be late in delivering the project on time. The same logic was extended after the construction was over, to the Metro train operations as Delhi Metro trains achieved over 99% punctuality on most days and if a train was even 60 seconds late, it was considered to have lost punctuality and was shown as a dead train.

This emphasis on punctuality has led to-

- Efficient and timely project delivery
- Punctuality in train operations
- The first phase of the project was completed 2 years 9 months ahead of the scheduled target by the DMRC as the Government had asked the DMRC to complete phase-I in 10 years while the DMRC was able to do it in 7 years and 3 months - a rare achievement for a Government project.
- In phase-II, the DMRC built 125 kms in only 4 ½ years beating their phase-I record also.

To ensure punctuality, the Delhi Metro has a master clock system which ensures that the same time is displayed at all its offices, control rooms and stations which ensures that the whole organization works with the same precision timing. The example for punctuality is set for the staff by the top management of DMRC and the culture flows from the top to the bottom. However, while everybody arrives for work at 9 am there is no insistence to sit late in the office beyond the scheduled 5.30 pm in the evening as it is felt that eight and a half hours are enough to complete your daily work provided you are concentrating on your work and are not wasting time in idle chit chatting, personal telephone conversations etc. during office hours.

Therefore, most DMRC officers and staff vacate the office premises between 5.30 to 6.30 PM in the evening. However, at construction sites and in maintenance, people work in shifts around the clock, keeping in view the construction schedule.

> *It was common for officers returning from foreign tours at 3 am or 4 am in the morning to be at work on the project site by 9 am the same day.*

Crisis Management

Taking moral responsibility for the Zamrudpur accident, Dr. E. Sreedharan tendered his resignation immediately.

NEXT नेक्स्ट
DIVYA PHYSIOTHERAPY & OCCUPATIONAL THERAPY CLINIC
Electrolux
AKAI
ONIDA
SAMSUNG
PHILIPS
DIVYA POLY CLINIC & DIAGNOSTIC CENTRE
DENTAL CLINIC
DIVYA POLY CLINIC
Onyx Financial Services
PRIME CRIME
DAVS
NEXT नेक्स्ट

DMRC has faced many crisis situations ever since the organisation began functioning effectively in 1997. The crash of the launcher at Laxmi Nagar construction site on 19th October, 2008 in which 2 persons were killed and 9 persons injured, followed by another crash of a launcher on 12th July, 2009 at Zamrudpur in which 7 people were killed and 15 were injured, are some of the major crisis situations that the DMRC handled. These were, infact, the first structural collapses that took place ever since DMRC began its construction activities on 1st October, 1998.

In Phase – I and Phase – II, there have been around 100 deaths but most of these incidents were caused by mistakes such as a person slipping or coming in the way of some construction machinery at the site such as a truck or a trailer reversing. There had been no situation where a huge structure came falling down, till the Laxmi Nagar crash in 2008. In the first instance, DMRC was able to effectively deal with the crisis by quickly briefing the press about the event and by taking measures to quickly remove the construction debris from the site. The same process was followed after the Zamrudpur accident also. Both these accidents happened at around 6 am on Sunday mornings.

In the Zamrudpur case, the Metro convened a full fledged Press Conference within a couple of hours of the accident on 12th July 2009, in which a prepared statement was read out giving the basic facts of the event which had happened namely, the type of accident, the suspected reason for the accident, the number of people killed and injured, their names and the hospitals where they had been shifted, including details of the interim compensation. At that stage, cross questioning was not allowed as DMRC did not have answers to all the queries, but this quick conference ensured that the basic information going out to the public through the media was uniform and correct. The Public Relations team had a tough time gathering this information internally, from the site and other sources in such a short time.

Another Press Conference was convened at 3 pm on the same day where the Managing Director announced his resignation in view of the accident. This led to a huge furore in the press and in the city with the Chief Minister insisting that Dr. Sreedharan withdraw his resignation. Ultimately, he was persuaded to withdraw his resignation.

The DMRC again keeping in view, its goodwill which it enjoyed from the public and the media in Delhi, was bouncing back from this crisis However, it was very unfortunate for the DMRC when on 13th July - the next day, one of the huge 400 tonne cranes, which were working simultaneously to lift the collapsed launching girder failed, and all the cranes came toppling down one after the other, resulting in massive chaos at the site. The huge steel structures fell all around with the TV crews and the media persons filming the recovery operations. Not only did the press have a very narrow escape but their cameras were able to capture the cranes falling down "LIVE" which proved to be excellent footage for the television channels – which was immediately telecast non stop 24X7. This did irreparable damage to Metro's image of being an efficient organization, which it had painstakingly built up over the last 10 years. Suddenly, the media became skeptical about the technical capability and safety procedures followed by the DMRC. With a hostile Press, questions were asked in the Parliament and emergency Board meetings were convened in which the representatives of the Delhi Government and the Central Government wanted to know how the DMRC will come out of this situation.

It took almost one year for the DMRC to emerge from this situation and this period was the most difficult time that the DMRC faced in handling the press, and external pressure groups during the entire period of Phase – I and Phase – II of the project. An interesting point was that public support still continued to be with DMRC as they were very happy with the Metro train services being provided to them and they felt that such accidents do happen during construction. The external forces again began to gather confidence in DMRC with the opening of NOIDA Metro line on 12th November 2009 and the Anand Vihar and Gurgaon lines on 6th January, 2010 and 21st June, 2010 respectively.

When everything went wrong
July, 2009

7 people died in Zamrudpur accident
Cranes collapsed at Zamrudpur
Metro Bhawan flooded with rain water...no electricity and ventilation for a week
78 year old Sreedharan had to climb 8 floors to reach his office daily

Cleanliness and Safety

Round the clock housekeeping services ensure a spotless and clean Metro system.

In DMRC, cleanliness is considered as Godliness. The Metro offices, work sites, station entrances are all supposed to be very clean and this culture is reflected from the Top Management in their inspection. The Managing Director keeps a sharp eye for cleanliness during all his inspections. It is not uncommon for him to wipe his finger against the floor of a Metro station or the Metro train to check the level of dirt there. The DMRC spends a lot of money in keeping cleaning parties and equipment at every Metro station. This is a constant battle since India is a country with a lot of heat, humidity, dust and population pressures with the public in the habit chewing and spitting pan which is difficult to clean. With a station every 1 km., keeping the Metro clean is a Herculean task as passengers bring street dirt whenever they come into the system. All trains are therefore, cleaned every night in the Metro maintenance depots after the closing of operations. Cleaning is also done during the night at the station.

Construction site areas are also required to be maintained properly with proper staging and placement of equipment with all material organized properly. Metro staff are supposed to be appropriately dressed and whenever they visit field construction sites they should wear their construction uniforms alongwith hard head gear and safety shoes apart from hi-visibility Jackets. In the office premises, the employees are expected to wear sober clothes and flashy or provocative dress is frowned upon by the Management. The Senior officers and supervisors are expected to set an example by dressing properly and maintaining a clean and smart appearance.

In the initial stages of DMRC, there was an instance when a foreign consultant in charge of safety, "Ian Carter" during a construction site inspection asked one of the Directors who was not wearing a safety shoe to avoid entering the site for safety reasons. The Director took it in proper spirit and returned after wearing safety shoes which were in his car parked closed by. The DMRC top management thus sets the standard for observance of safety regulations at Metro construction sites.

TS#02

NO VEHICLE
MOVEMENT
ALLOWED IN
WASHING BAY
ACCEPT TRAIN
NO OTHER
VEHICLES ARE
ALLOW TO
MOVE IN
WASHING BAY.

The Pace of Construction

Phase I – 65 kms completed in 7 years 9 months
(2 years 3 months ahead of schedule)
Phase II – 125 kms completed in a record time of 4 ½ years

The fast pace of Metro construction in Delhi is indeed remarkable, keeping in view the difficulties of working in an urban environment where one has to work under restricted conditions with buildings all around and water lines, sewer lines, telephone cables, electric cables etc. laid all along with heavy road traffic and population pressures. In comparison, similar construction activities in barren or rural areas becomes much easier as construction in urban surroundings requires working within tightly restricted access areas because the land is just not available to work freely.

In addition, in a democratic country like India, the work can be restricted or held up by people going to the Court of Law and therefore, the process of land acquisition has to be handled carefully, especially when private properties are involved. Another difficulty in working in a democratic system like India are the bureaucratic procedures and rules as cutting down even a single tree in Delhi requires permission from many different departments and at times it took almost 10 months of chasing before DMRC was granted tree cutting permission in some of the cases. DMRC has cut over 30,000 trees for the project, so the amount of file chasing that was done to get these permissions from the different government agencies can easily be imagined. This required constant chasing without which the Project would have been delayed.

In countries like China which have a different system of governance, the Metro expansion is happening very fast but China has the advantage that once the decision is taken to implement the project, they do not have to face difficulty which the DMRC had to face in land acquisition, rehabilitation of the project affected persons and getting necessary clearances and permissions before starting the work. The DMRC had to cut through the red tape which was not easy.

Construction projects in a city like Delhi require clearances from the Delhi Urban Art Commission, Central Vista Commission, Delhi Development Authority, New Delhi Municipal Council, Municipal Corporation of Delhi, Archaeological Survey of India, Forest Department, Fire Brigade etc. depending upon the area or activity involved. Utility owning agencies such as the Mahanagar Telephone Nigam, Delhi Jal Board, BSES, NDPL (Electricity) also have to give their clearance.

To save time, DMRC itself took upon the responsibility of diverting the utilities rather than waiting for respective agencies to divert them.

Metro engineers have been stoned, pushed,locked up and threatened with being burnt when they went to acquire land for the project. In Khyber Pass, where the Metro train depot is situated today, in one instance Mr. Daljeet Singh, then Dy. Chief Engineer(Land) was stoned by truck drivers who tried to set him and his car ablaze in 1999. Similar cases happened at Chawri Bazaar, Tilak Nagar and Boulevard Road in Phase-I. Inspite of this, land was acquired on time through grit and determination.

A Profitable Metro

DMRC has been making operational profit since Day 1 of its operations.

Mass Rapid Transport Systems are very capital intensive in their construction period and therefore, out of the 140 odd Metros in the world, none of them make an overall profit, though 5 Metros namely the Singapore, Hong kong, Taipei, Tokyo and Delhi Metro are making an operational profit. Operational profit means that the daily earnings exceed the expenditure incurred by the organisation everyday. DMRC has a very healthy operational ratio of 0.52 currently which means that for every rupee that the company earns, it spends only 0.52 paisa on its expenditure.

DMRC is a profitable venture due to the following reasons:

1) A large portion of the Delhi Metro is elevated and this has minimised the cost of construction as underground construction costs almost two and a half times more than that of an elevated Metro construction. In addition, underground sections require constant ventilation and air conditioning arrangements which inflates the cost of operating an underground station to twice than that of an elevated station. Keeping this in view, DMRC decided to go elevated except in the areas which were extremely populated and in the Central and Southern parts of the city.

2) DMRC earns about 20% of its daily revenue from non operational sources such as Property Development which includes revenues earned from commercial advertisements, shop rentals and stand-alone projects such as the Information Technology Park which has been built by DMRC at Shastri Park. DMRC has followed the Hong kong Metro Model in this aspect as just passenger fares are never enough to sustain a Metro system.

3) Staff cost normally constitutes a very heavy chunk of organsational expenditure and therefore, DMRC decided to adopt international standards in this regard by going for building automated technical systems which required less staff deployment. This can be seen in the Metro trains in Delhi, where there is only one Train Operator (TO). Over all, DMRC employs about 37 persons for every km of the Metro with a staff strength of over 7,000 for a route length of 190 kms. This is comparable to the staff ratios of Singapore Metro which is considered the most efficient in this regard. The DMRC has also outsourced non-operational and non-safety requirements such as cleanliness of the Metro system and token vending at Station counters which are handled by private contractors. Security is also largely a state responsibility in DMRC and is handled by the Central Industrial Security Force (CISF).

McDonald's
FAMILY RESTAURANT

Partnerships

Contractors are considered as partners in the progress of DMRC

The credit for the successful completion of the Delhi Metro Project also goes to the contractors executing the work and the financial assistance received by the DMRC from the Japanese Government. All major contracts in DMRC are awarded after international competitive bidding through open advertisements in the newspapers. In the first stage, contractors are invited for pre-qualification so that the DMRC can check whether the contractor is technically and financially capable of executing the work. All the contractors who pre-qualify in their respective fields are then permitted to bid for the main contract on an even footing. This ensures that DMRC gets capable contractors who are able to deliver the goods. Therefore, apart from the cost and the technical capability, the past record etc. of the contractor is also gauged to ensure that the contractors provide good quality of work as per the expectations of the organization.

To encourage indigenization and self sufficiency within India, in many international contracts involving Joint Ventures, DMRC has always encouraged association of an Indian partner or company so that these contractors gain relevant experience in their respective fields in their association with the foreign contractors. Today, the country is more or less self sufficient in Civil Engineering though deficiencies for critical items continue in the field of rolling stock, signaling and telecommunication. Foreign companies such as Bombardier have set up manufacturing units in India and Metro trains are being manufactured at Savli in Gujrat. Earlier, Bharat Earth Movers Limited (BEML), a public sector company had tied up with ROTEM of Korea and Mitsubishi, Japan, to make Metro coaches in Bangalore. DMRC, which is the first Metro in the world to start the use of contact less tokens for single journey initially used to import them from Sony, Japan, at a cost of ₹ 90 approximately per token in 2002. Today, these tokens are being made in India and each costs only ₹ 20 approximately to DMRC. Indian companies such as Larsen and Toubro, Hindustan Construction Company, Gammon etc. have emerged as major players coming forward for Metro construction projects in India, with the experience they have gained in the construction of the Delhi Metro Project.

The Government of Japan extended crucial financial assistance to the Metro Project in Delhi through a soft loan. The initial financial and technical assistance for Delhi Metro during 1996-97 was extended by Overseas Economic Cooperation Fund (OECF) of Japan. On Oct. 01, 1999, the OECF merged with Export Import Bank of Japan to become Japan Bank for International Cooperation (JBIC). During Oct. 01, 2008, JBIC's ODA Loan operations merged with Japan International Cooperation Agency. Presently, JICA India is headed by Mr. Shinichi Yamanaka, Chief Representative. The loan from JICA was given to DMRC at an interest rate of

Crane
S.ML
2007

KRUPP
KMK 6180

about 1.3%, which had to be paid back over a period of 30 years with a 10 year moratorium for pay back, which meant that no payment would be made for the first 10 years after taking each tranche of the loan. The loan was taken in tranches i.e in installments from JICA depending upon the requirement of money for DMRC. The agreement for the loan was made between the Government of Japan and the Government of India (Ministry of Finance) and the Government of India guaranteeing the entire amount. In addition, the Government of the India also agreed to take care of any fluctuations in the currency exchange rates so that the burden on DMRC was not increased due to the same, keeping in view the fluctuation of the Indian rupee with reference to the Japanese Yen.

The Delhi Metro Rail Corporation (DMRC) has paid back an amount of ₹ 826.50 crores to the Japan International Cooperation Agency (JICA) already.

The first tranche for Phase – I and Phase – II was received by DMRC in 1998 and 2006 respectively. The last tranche for Phase – I was received in 2005. The 4th tranche of Phase – II was sanctioned in 2009 while the final (5th) tranche was received in 2010. Overall, the JICA has collectively paid over ₹ 16,000 crores to DMRC for both Phase – I and Phase – II project. The DMRC maintained a close link with JICA throughout Phase-I and Phase-II with Mr. M.P.Singh, Additional Chief Development Specialist (JICA) closely monitoring the progress of the Delhi Metro Project throughout.

DMRC started paying back the loan for Phase – I (1st tranche) and the interest amount in the year 2007. The total loan paid back for Phase – I is ₹ 129.55 crores and the interest on the loan amount for both Phase – I & II has been paid back to the tune of ₹ 696.95 crores.

The DMRC is one of the few Metros in the world making an operational profit and the surplus generated is used to payback the loan taken from the Government of Japan. The DMRC does not depend upon any subsidy and is not a financial burden through efficient management and optimum sizing of the organization.

For Phase III, the JICA is expected to sanction approximately 53 % of the Project cost. The first tranche amounting to more than ₹ 6900 crores is expected to be sanctioned by first quarter of 2012. The total cost for Phase III in Delhi will be ₹ 35,242 crores.

"We wanted to ensure that not only competent contractors were considered for the project, but also all of them could fairly compete. In this PSU, the approach is that you pre-qualify a very limited number of contractors and invite bids from them. That approach ensures that we have sufficient number of quality bidders, with good track record. Those who pre-qualify are given total flexibility of making joint ventures with foreign partners, which was required to bring in the required knowledge, capital and access to technology. So, the process was such that it ensured we had sufficient number of highly qualified contractors, who were interested in our project. We supplied them the information they required, so that they were able to deliver their bids. These qualification criteria were developed within the ambit of Central Vigilance Commission guidelines.

When we received a large number of interested bidders, after detailed evaluation those pre-qualified only were invited to bid for projects. Then we used to go for detailed technical evaluation of the bids, where we took note of various requirements like safety records and timeliness of delivery. Attention was given to internal competencies of the bidding organizations. i.e. whether they had good teams. Financial strength of the company also used to be a requirement, but to ensure that the technically competent companies would not suffer because of mandatory requirements of having higher cash flow (turnover) requirements, we encouraged joint ventures. Thus, a company with higher financial strength could join one with higher technical strengths, like the airport line where technical qualification was procured from a foreign partner and financial qualification from Reliance Ambani group. Sometimes, we also helped contractors find suitable partners, so that DMRC could benefit"

Chief Engineer (Tender), DMRC in conversation with the Indian Institute of Management, Ahmedabad*

* Delhi Metro Excellence: in Management - UNDP, IIM Ahemdabad and Delhi Metro Rail Corporation Ltd.

Systems - Vigilance & Audit

An independent vigilance department is guiding DMRC towards a corruption free organisation.

Though the DMRC has worked very fast it continued to follow all the rules , regulations and practices which are followed by government departments and public sector units in dealing with all vigilance cases within the organisation. A Schedule of Powers was drawn up delegating powers commensurate with their role and responsibility to different level of officers so that they could take quick decisions on important matters.

The DMRC is considered as a Government undertaking like a Public Sector Unit (PSU) since it was owned 50% by the Government of NCT of Delhi and 50% by the Government of India and all the procedures of audit and vigilance are available in DMRC. There is an internal and external audit apart from a permanent audit body stationed in the organization and the DMRC is subject to the scrutiny of the Comptroller and Auditor General (CAG) whose report is submitted to the Parliament. All audit objections and queries have to be replied to by the DMRC .

The DMRC also has an independent Vigilance organization which is headed by the Chief Vigilance Officer and all rules and regulations and safeguards prescribed by the Chief Vigilance Commission (CVC) are followed by DMRC.

However, the DMRC has a very practical approach and even though some decisions may have been taken in a haste keeping in view the timely completion of the project the DMRC didn't believe in witch hunting if it felt that the intention of the person was not wrong. Thus, the management approach was to check the genuiness of the intention and the Public interests and convenience while coming to a decision.

The personal example and high standards set by the Managing Director in personal integrity acted as a guiding force for all the Metro managers .

The DMRC is a new organization and deals with the public in large numbers as they travel as passengers on the Metro System. As such the normal procedures of the Government had to be adapted for carrying out system improvement measures. At the same time, the Vigilance Department had to ensure that the internal morale and motivation of the Metro employees was not dampened by these measures.

The confidence of the public and handling of their complaints also required adequate checks and proper care for the good public image of the organization.

The Chief Vigilance Officer of the organization is easily accessible to the public and holds meetings with DMRC site engineers and operational staff to train them about sensitivity on vigilance matters. Contractors are also encouraged to interact with him regularly. Shri S.C.Jindal, the current CVO encourages positive interaction with DMRC staff and gives inputs regularly to disseminate regular flow of information to avoid making mistakes in day to day working.

ACME'S
Champion

Environment

Delhi Metro plants 10 trees for every single tree cut during construction.

The Delhi Metro Project took special care of environmental issue as DMRC was always aware that this was a sensitive issue which could badly delay the project if it is not handled properly. Thus, in the Detailed Project Report (DPR) itself there was a Environmental Impact Assessment (EIA) study done for the project and the Ministry of Environment and Forest were involved at that stage.

The DMRC had to cut about 30 thousand trees in Phase-I and II of the project and a commitment was made to the Government by DMRC that the organisation would plant 10 trees as compensatory afforestation which was further increased to plant 11 trees for every tree cut in Phase-II. The actual compensatory afforestation was done by the Forest Department of the Government of Delhi and the funding was done by the DMRC. The DMRC also agreed to pay for the up keep of these saplings for a period of 3 years so that these trees gain sufficient strength and would survive in the long run. However, this compensatory afforestation was done mostly in the outlying areas of Delhi like Najafgarh as open land was scarce in the central parts of the city. In Phase-II, DMRC decided to plant at least one of these trees near the location from where the original tree was cut so that the local environment remained intact.

DMRC also transplanted a number of these trees which were eco-friendly and had good chance of survival after transplantation. These trees had to be transplanted within a radius of 5 kms from where they were originally located and this was done through a specialized agency which was experienced in such work as the trees had to be carefully excavated, chemically treated and delicately transplanted to the new location. Some of the sites where they were transplanted include the Delhi Zoological Park, Talkatora Gardens, Shastri Park, Janpath, etc.

DMRC also received ISO 14001 and OHSAS 18001 certification for environmental protection and for the good environmental practices followed at its construction sites. The New York Metro was also associated in the environmental efforts initially with DMRC.

DMRC also became the first Railway System in the world to receive Carbon Credits for regenerative braking as DMRC trains save 33% of the energy lost during the braking process. This is reconverted into energy and reused in the system. This saving has been converted into Carbon Credits by DMRC. DMRC has also earned Carbon Credits as the 1.8 million passengers who travel on the Metro today are saving carbon emissions which would have otherwise been released in the atmosphere had they travelled by buses, cars, two wheelers etc.

The Delhi Metro Rail Corporation has been certified by the United Nations (UN) as the first metro rail and Rail based system in the world to get carbon credits for reducing Green

House Gas Emissions as it has helped to reduce pollution levels in the city by 6.3 lakh tons every year thus, helping in reducing global warming.

DMRC has helped in reduction in emission of harmful gases into the city's atmosphere and the United Nations Body administering the Clean Development Mechanism (CDM) under the Kyoto Protocol has certified that DMRC has reduced emissions and, thus, earned carbon credits worth about ₹ 47 crore annually for the next seven years starting 2007and with the increase in number of passengers, this figure will increase.

No other Metro in the world could get Carbon Credits for the above because of the very stringent requirement of the United Nations Body to provide conclusive documentary proof of reduction in emissions. It is difficult to give documentary proof of the difference of energy consumption of two scenarios, i.e. "With Metro and Without Metro". DMRC proposed an innovative method of proving the emissions using sampling techniques. After rigorous persuasion, the UN body finally agreed with this technique as the technique is very scientific in nature.

This is the second CDM project from DMRC to be registered with the UN body in the last three years. DMRC's first CDM project on regenerative braking had also achieved many international firsts, apart from earning valuable foreign exchange for the country. Environmental safety education was given to all DMRC contractual workers at its construction sites throughout the project and all its contract conditions contain a SHE manual (Safety, Health and Environmental manual) which the contractors are supposed to follow during the execution of their works.

Economic Rate of Return

A journalist claimed that he saves ₹ 18,000 a month by travelling in the Metro in place of his personal vehicle.

Metro projects are very capital intensive and can be justified only on their high economic rate of returns since these projects provide a number of social and economical benefits to the citizens as they save time in their travel. They enjoy better health because of less exposure to poisonous automobile fumes and the accidents are less since the Metro is safer than road transport. Some of these benefits were quantified by DMRC with the help of the Central Road Research Institute (CRRI) in 2006, the main findings of which has been enumerated below:-

Economic Benefits of Delhi Metro in 2011

Benefit in Crore Rupees (₹)	Year 2011
Annual time cost saved of Metro Passengers	2978.08
Annual fuel cost saved of Metro passengers	523.81
Annual vehicle (Capital and Operating) cost saved	758.70
Emission saving cost	80.92
Accident cost	27.70
Annual time cost saved of road passengers	197.57
Annual fuel cost saved of road passengers	23.87
Annual Infrastructure Maintenance cost	314.88
Total cost of all benefits (Cost without discount)	4,905.54

In terms of the quantitative benefits also, Delhi Metro has played a stellar role. On an average, Delhi Metro has helped remove more than 1.5 lakh vehicles from the roads of Delhi daily and has played a role in preventing more than two lakh tonnes of emissions of harmful gases. Let us have a look at the quantitative benefits derived by the city of Delhi due to the Delhi Metro:

Quantitative Benefits	Year 2011
Daily vehicles of the road	1,59,170
All Accidents saved	660
Fatal Accidents Saved	132
Emissions Prevented	In Tonnes
CO2	2,83,717
CO	5456

लिफ्ट Lift
लिफ्ट Lift

HC	2376
NOX	1292
PM	182
SO2	13
Total Emission Saved	2,93,035

If the social and economic benefits are quantified, then the value of accrued benefits of Phase-I will become ₹ 10,801.64 crores by the end of March 2012, while the cost of construction of Phase-I was ₹ 10,571 crores.

In addition, with the number of commuters on the Delhi Metro rising, the environmental and social benefits gained by the National Capital because of the mass transport system will help recover the full cost of Phase-I, two years earlier than anticipated by the Central Road Research Institute (CRRI).

According to the study by CRRI, the break-even of the cost of Phase-I has already been achieved by December 2011. CRRI had carried out a similar study in 2007 when it had concluded that the cost of Phase I would be recovered by 2013.

The financial rate of return of Metro projects had never been high and that is one of the reasons why private parties do not enter into Metro construction unless they are given some 'sweeteners' to bolster their revenue. Therefore, most Metros world over are funded through government sources since the main benefits of the Metro comes to the city and the public.

An example illustrates this point :

A journalist in one of the press conferences mentioned that he is saving ₹ 18, 000 per month with the opening of the NOIDA Metro line as this gentleman who was staying in Subhash Nagar on Line-3 earlier used to commute upto NOIDA by his own car which used to cost him around ₹ 20,000 per month which included the fuel cost, salary to the driver etc. However with the opening of the NOIDA corridor, he is now able to take Metro from the Subhash Nagar Metro Station to NOIDA which costs him only ₹ 2,000 per month. This saving of ₹ 18,000, however, was going to this individual journalist as his personal financial benefit and was not coming to DMRC. As he stopped using his own vehicle, the city's pollution level decreased and in addition, probable accidents were also avoided.

Outsourcing

Outsourcing the non critical works help DMRC in forming a lean but efficient work force.

Exit
Handbag, Briefcase,
Tiffin Box etc.

Life Insurance &
Pension Plans
HDFC
STANDARD LIFE
Sar Utha Ke Jiyo
Power
Up

With the objective of maintaining a lean and efficient work force, completely focused towards ensuring quality Metro services, the DMRC has outsourced some non-critical operations and maintenance areas to specialized agencies. This has helped the organization to save on long term manpower and financial liabilities.

As part of this policy, some operation related activities such as dispensing of tokens, cleaning of Metro trains and stations etc have been handed over to private agencies which provide DMRC with trained professionals to carry out these assignments. However, the DMRC personnel keep a very close eye on the quality of service provided by these agencies and strict disciplinary action is initiated if any dereliction of duty is reported.

In addition, the security of Delhi Metro is handled largely by the state (the Central Industrial Security Force & Delhi Police) and some support is provided by DMRC through private security agencies, mostly the Group 4 Securitas agency.

This policy of outsourcing has saved DMRC from the burden of incurring additional financial liability of providing provident fund, medical expenses etc. Other human resource related liabilities related to recruitment procedures, leave issues etc have also been avoided and the HR department has been able to concentrate on the recruitment and training of the staff related to the core activities of the organisation.

However, the DMRC has outsourced only-non critical activities and did not touch operational areas, especially safety related matters, as the lives of the passengers were involved in these areas.

In spite of using mechanical gadgetry for cleaning the Metro stations, the DMRC has to dedicate atleast 25 to 30 persons at every station who work round the clock in shifts to ensure that the stations are constantly cleaned. In summer months and during the monsoons, people enter the stations with dirt and dust on their shoes which are rubbed off inside the station platforms and concourse.

Thus in Delhi's hot and humid conditions, almost four thousand people are involved in keeping the Metro clean. Therefore, had this activity not been outsourced, the DMRC would have been burdened tremendously both from the business and management perspective.

This outsourcing policy has also set an example of competent human resource management for all other public sector establishments which suffer from the malaise of over staffing.

Delegation of Powers

The MD is vested with all the necessary powers to execute the project without any interference.

SIDWAL

DMRC's Top Management

Dr. E. Sreedharan
Ex-Managing Director

Mr. Mangu Singh
Managing Director

Mr. Satish Kumar
Director/Electrical

Mr. R.N. Joshi
Director/Finance

Mr. Raj Kumar
Director/Operations

Mr. H.S. Anand
Director/Rolling Stock

Mr. Kumar Keshav
Director/Project & Planning

Mr. Jitendra Tyagi
Director (Works)
(Not in Picture)

One of the reasons why DMRC was able to execute its work quickly was that all powers of the management board have been vested in the post of the Managing Director of DMRC who has been empowered to take final decisions on all matters. All tenders irrespective of their value were decided by the Managing Director and very high value tenders were put up to the Board of Directors for information and ratification subsequently. Thus, DMRC lost no time in settling even big value tenders which were decided quickly by the management itself.

The DMRC management took a number of bold decisions during the execution of the project such as start of the work on the Shahdara – Tis Hazari section even before the sanction of the loan from JICA which was slightly delayed due to the fallout of the Pokhran Nuclear blast by India. But the Metro authorities decided to launch construction of the Shahdara- Tis Hazari section on 1st of October 1998 utilizing the funds available as equity.

The DMRC on its own also decided to reduce the implementation time of the Phase-I project from 10 years to 7 years unilaterally to save on cost as each day's delay would mean that the cost of the project would go up because of inflation. Ultimately DMRC was able to complete the work in 7 years and 9 months. Thus, DMRC saved 2 years 3 months from the original schedule of 10 years given by the Government.

In Phase-II also, DMRC took many such bold decisions which facilitated the construction of 125 kilometers of Metro lines in only four and a half years.

The delegation of full powers to the Managing Director in Delhi Metro Rail Corporation (DMRC) helped the organisation in taking bold and firm decisions. As a result of this, in the initial stages of the project (1999-2000), the DMRC was able to offload the work of the construction of a Metro station at Tis Hazari from a public sector construction company and awarded a fresh contract immediately to a private company since the PSU performance was not upto the mark. Subsequently, DMRC cancelled contracts at other locations also, where it felt that the contractors would not be able to deliver satisfactorily and on time.

Speed of Decisions

Delay in taking decisions was frowned upon and even wrong decisions were acceptable, but delays were not acceptable.

Qutab Minar
कुतुब मीनार
Qutab Minar

In DMRC, it is possible to get a decision on the same day. The top management is always accessible in crucial matters and can be approached during office hours for taking decisions. Even after office hours, it is possible to get verbal approval on urgent matters irrespective of the time of the day and go ahead with the work. Subsequently, written ratification can be taken.

The delay in taking decisions was frowned upon and even wrong decisions were acceptable but delays were not acceptable. The pressure on deadlines was always maintained throughout the construction period and the same is witnessed in the punctuality of the train operations.

The fast decision making can be seen as even major tenders were decided sometimes in 18 – 19 days. In procurement areas also, the DMRC is known to be very fast and as a result of which, other departments such as the fire department of Delhi Government asked DMRC to purchase their equipment through DMRC. Thus, the hazmat (hazardous materials) vehicle of the fire department was procured by DMRC for them instead of the fire department procuring it directly for themselves. Other departments in Delhi also approached DMRC from time to time to purchase their equipment through DMRC which is known for fast clearance in the matter.

Speedy decisions are also ensured during the Head of Departments meeting where bottlenecks, delay and decisions are analyzed and corrected on a weekly basis.

Metro site engineers are encouraged to give immediate project & construction related decisions to the contractors immediatly on site itself to avoid any delay in project work

The Managing Director openly used to encourage officers to bring their files and issues to him for a decision. On many occasions, when issues could not be decided between different departments, he would ask for the papers to be brought to him directly and would give a clear-cut decision on the matter. This helped in speeding up the decision making process and encouraged the Heads of Departments also to take quick decisions.

Some of these decisions helped in huge financial savings also as during one of the initial site inspections of the Managing Director between Shahdara and Tis Hazari he decided to build the Metro on the embankment rather than having it elevated between Shahdara and Seelampur, thus, saving hundreds of crores by this single spot decision during the inspection.

Inspection of construction sites by the MD and Directors on Christmas, Eid, Diwali and Holidays was a common feature as every day was important to give decisions on time.

Consultancy

DMRC has emerged as the main consultant for all Metro projects across the country.

The Delhi Metro also has a national objective of spreading the Metro culture in the rest of the country keeping in view the rapid urbanisation in India.

As the Metro is the only means of urban transportation which can carry upto 90,000 passangers per hour per direction, the DMRC felt that it was the ideal transport solution for cities such as Chennai, Bengaluru, Mumbai, Ahemdabad, Kolkata, Pune etc. and with this aim in mind, the DMRC provided consultancy to all cities in India which needed Metros at very reasonable cost.

In the initial stages, the DMRC had to incur quite a bit of expenditure to get the latest technology available in the world in the field of Metro...

- Signal Engineering
- Rolling Stock Engineering
- Civil Engineering
- Electrical Engineering
- Telecommunication Engineering etc.

As a result of absorbing these technologies, DMRC became the main consultant for cities planning Metros in India. Thus valuable foreign exchange for the country was saved as otherwise, these cities would have had to go abroad to get these technologies.

Rather than remaining confined to the boundaries of the National Capital Region, DMRC is now spreading its wings across the country, providing consultancy and guidance to all the other upcoming Metro projects in India and even abroad. In fact, in Jaipur, DMRC is carrying out the construction of a 9.25 kilometers of Metro lines for the Jaipur Metro.

DMRC's work culture and project implementation expertise has gained so much appreciation that it has even bagged consultancy as well as construction projects beyond the realms of Metro railway.

DMRC has adopted the latest technologies in construction, signaling, rolling stock, track, fare collection, power supply, ventilation, air conditioning etc. The Metro system in Delhi runs with the latest signaling system with Automatic Train Protection (ATP) & Automatic Train Operating Systems (ATO) monitored by centralized Operations Control Centres (OCCs).

Today, DMRC is in a position to advise which technology would be most suitable for various cities planning rail-based solutions for urban transportation. DMRC has a fully contact-less ticketing system. It was the world's first Metro to introduce contact-less tokens which have now been adopted by the HongKong, Bangkok and Taipei Metros.

DMRC's operating systems are among the most efficient in the world and the trains have a punctuality of almost 100% which has been possible because of the high standards of maintenance. DMRC has also established world-class training facilities and has its own training school and top-of-the-line simulators are installed for training the train operators.

Because of its work culture, DMRC is an example of how urban transportation interventions should be executed so that they can be completed within time and cost estimates. The meticulous care in designing the Delhi Metro system has enabled DMRC to be one of the very few Metros in the world to make operational profits and till date the Delhi Metro does not depend upon government subsidies for its operation and maintenance.

Low cost: DMRC's experts are all from the country itself and, therefore, their cost is low as compared to expatriate foreign experts. The cost of consultancy service required by DMRC, therefore, is very low as compared to other international consultants. This is particularly relevant for developing countries where the cost of expatriate experts is very high.

Quality: DMRC's experience and expertise is very relevant to the developing countries. DMRC's recommendations, therefore, are prone to be more reliable and bankable in those countries.

Today, Delhi Metro is visited regularly by personnel wanting to understand how and what makes DMRC tick. The management techniques of this organization have aroused the curiosity of the Indian Army, the Administrative Service, Harvard University, Wharton Yale and the Darden School of Management apart from a host of other public sector and allied organizations.

DMRC's consultancy purview today no longer remains confined to preparation of the Detailed Project Reports (DPRs) for Metro systems in various Indian cities. The reputation it has earned because of the efficient project management in Delhi has won the respect of authorities nationwide. Today, DMRC is involved as a prime consultant to some of India's upcoming Metro projects. It is pertinent to note that although Kolkata developed India's first Metro project almost a decade before the Delhi Metro, it has turned to DMRC for its expansion.

As the prime consultant, DMRC will advise these Metro corporations regarding tender documents, including estimates, render expert advice on various technical matters including system selections, various specifications of engineering works and finalizing security systems, assist and advice in finalizing operation and maintenance strategy, training programmes etc.

The Delhi Metro project is today seen as a model of how urban transport systems can be successfully built in crowded cities. Visitors from the US, Europe, Japan, South East Asia, South Asia, Australia, Africa etc., have toured the system to understand DMRC's project management techniques and technologies used.

DMRC has completed its first international consultancy assignment, a Special Assistance on Project Implementation (SAPI) study for the Jakarta Mass Rapid Transit (MRT) System in Indonesia. Various discussions have also been held with other countries such as Ireland, Pakistan, Sri Lanka, Bangladesh, Syria and Vietnam who have expressed interest in DMRC's expertise in developing their own Metro systems.

DMRC is the pioneer in urban tunneling projects in India and because of its rich experience in this area, it has been involved in three prestigious road projects in Delhi which require tunneling work. The first construction project completed by DMRC is the Northern Access Road to the Indira Gandhi International Airport which was a design & construct project. This road connection is partly underground, under the flight path of a runway.

DMRC's track record in timely completion of projects has ensured that its skills are sought after not only for transport-related projects but also for infrastructure development in other areas. Let us take a look:

DMRC has built Delhi's first world class 'Information Technology Park' near the Shastri Park Metro Station. It is an intelligent and fully air conditioned building equipped with several facilities and state-of-the-art technical systems.

DMRC has completed and commissioned an underground multi-level automated parking complex for the Delhi High Court, one of the first such projects in the national capital. The five-level complex has an area of about 9,862 sq.m. and can accommodate 1,500 cars. The complex is fully automated with the latest technology and equipment, CCTVs and full electricity back up for the safety and security of cars.

The Delhi Government's Directorate of Health Services has appointed DMRC as the project management consultant for the construction of Phase-II of the city's ultra-modern, super-specialty Institute of Liver and Biliary Sciences. The project, covers 83,655 sq.m. and has an academic block, a clinical block and residential blocks, besides others.

The DMRC spread the Metro culture in India by visits of the MD to Chennai, Bengaluru, Mumbai, Kolkatta, Ahemdabad, Pune, Ludhiana, Bhopal..every Saturday and Sunday to meet the Chief Ministers and Chief Secretaries to convince them of the need to have a metro system in their cities. Weekends were chosen so that Metro work in Delhi did not suffer.

Balancing Different Streams

Moulding departmental interests to meet organisational objectives always remained supreme for DMRC

The departments of Delhi Metro have been formed on the basis of patterns available in the Indian Railways and, thus, there are separate departments for signaling and telecommunication, electrical, rolling stock, civil engineering, stores, personnel, general administration, accounts and finance, public relations, legal etc. Officers belonging to these streams are posted either in the Project Department i.e. those involved in the construction of the Delhi Metro or in Operations and Maintenance i.e. those involved in running of the trains.

The departmentalization of officers and staff has its own advantage as it enables people to specialize in their respective streams. However, it has its own inherent disadvantages also as there is a tendency to think compartmentally and departmentally. Thus, departmental interests sometimes tend to outweigh organizational interest and people tend to become narrow in their focus as they start concentrating on goals and interests of their respective departments only.

The task before the top management in-particular the Managing Director, was thus, to mould these different departmental interests in such a fashion that organizational interests were always supreme. Departmental bickering could be seen even at the highest levels and the organizational focus was visible more at the level of the Managing Director.

Even in the construction field, the DMRC witnessed the same as in DMRC there is a concept of having a Chief Project Manager (CPM) who would be overall in charge of all aspects pertaining to the construction of a particular route. The CPM is normally a civil engineer and he is supposed to answer all aspects pertaining to the construction of his line including electrical, signaling, telecommunication, track etc. However, in practice, it is difficult for the CPM to be very effective in his coordination with other departments apart from his own i.e. civil engineering. The concept of the CPM however, is working well as inspite of inter departmental friction, the Delhi Metro has been able to commission Metro Lines on promised dates. However, the CPMs received good backing, freedom, independence in working and the support of the top management for proper execution of the assigned project.

In Phase-I, the three lines under construction were given to three different CPMs whereas in Phase-II, all six lines were given to six different CPMs whose number was increased subsequently. Thus, each CPM was required to focus on his line alone with his own specific task in mind. Thus, even though the DMRC had to construct double the number of kilometers in Phase-II, they were able to do the same by simply sub-dividing the work among equal number of sub-components or equal number of CPMs.

In one category i.e. that of the Train Drivers who are called as Train Operators in DMRC, it was decided to merge this cadre with that of the Station Controller's (popularly understood as Station Masters of Indian Railways). In the Indian Railways Train Drivers are a separate cadre and the Station Masters belong to a different stream and there is no interchangeability between these cadres. However, DMRC decided to merge eligibility of the Train Operators and the Station Controllers thus reducing the vulnerability of the Metro administration in case of any strike by the Drivers (Train Operators). This was a very wise decision and in emergency situations the Station Manager/Station Controllers have been able to drive the Trains in case the existing Train Operator faced any problem. Thus, common training and promotional avenues are provided for the Train Operators and the Station Controllers.

Another issue faced by the DMRC Management pertained to balancing the pressures and interests of different groups of individuals who had come on deputation from different organizations such as the Indian Railways, CPWD, Delhi Jal Board, Sports Authority of India, Konkan Railway etc. and with those persons recruited directly by DMRC. There were issues pertaining to their seniority which were difficult to balance out and many of these issues are still persisting within the organization. Draft policies have been made in this regard but as usual it is difficult to satisfy all the interest groups equally.

The Former President of India Dr. APJ Abdul Kalam felt that the Delhi Metro Rail Project has given to the nation the potential of executing a fast transport system using high technology with reliability through a time bound mission. Dr. Kalam said that DMRC was able to ensure that all scheduled sections were completed by the target dates or before and within their respective budgets through the proper management skills of the Managing Director, Dr. E.Sreedharan.

AFCONS
NAVAYUGA

Customer Care

DMRC staff are given an orientation to focus on customers as they are extremely important in our customer service.

The DMRC staff are given an orientation to focus on customers as they are extremely important in our customer service. In most of the government organizations, the government servants hardly believe that they are servants but rather feel as if the people are their servants. This attitude of lethargy, arrogance and complacency is extremely dangerous for an organisation and can be quite disastrous for its image also as people tend to resent such organisations and with this in focus the Metro staff is given customer orientation and special training in customer etiquettes and behavior especially for frontline Metro Staff posted at Metro Stations. In fact, some of the staff who are designated as Customer Relations Assistants (CRAs) are posted at the Customer Care Counters.

DMRC also provides training in First Aid in coordination with the St. John Ambulance Association to its entire staff at its training school at Shastri Park. This training is very useful as the Metro Staff respond very positively and quickly whenever there is a medical emergency at a Metro Station or inside a train. Wheelchairs and stretchers are available at all stations and the DMRC has tied-up with nearby local hospitals for the treatment of such passengers. In extreme cases where the passenger is not accompanied by anybody known to him then a Metro staff accompanies the passenger to the nearby hospital and remains there till a family member of the passenger arrives.

A system of receiving public complaints through the Delhi Metro feedback mechanism on its official website www.delhimetrorail.com is available apart from complaint books at every Metro Station. A Public Complaint Officer has also been designated to handle Public Complaints from the Operations and Maintenance Department of the DMRC.

The Delhi Metro Rail Corporation recently installed Powerheart Automated External Defibrillators (AEDs) at its two biggest interchange stations i.e, Central Secretariat and Kashmere Gate Metro Stations which will be of immense use to help save the life of a person suffering a Sudden Cardiac Arrest (SCA) as the heart stops functioning in such a case and without cardiopulmonary resuscitation from someone, brain damage or death can occur in just four to six minutes. The most effective emergency treatment

6
BOMBARDIER

6
6727
34
29

for SCA is use of public access defibrillation or AEDs to resuscitate a victim's heart until proper medical help arrives. These AEDs send an electric shock to the heart and allow it to return to a normal rhythm. AEDs can be used even by non-medical personnel.

Anticipating trouble on the first day of commercial operations on 25th December 2002 the PR Department of DMRC trained and hired young college students (called sahayaks) to help the public use escalators, handle the sophisticated Fare collection system (AFC) and to use the modern trains. It was these 300 odd youngsters who held the Metro system together on 25th December, 2002 as lakhs of people thronged to use the Metro on the first day in Delhi when technical systems were not working as per plan. The DMRC system was under pressure but held.

Personal Fitness

Yoga and meditation habits are inculcated in the employees to keep them healthy and in sound mind.

Good Health is essential if a person has to perform well at his job. To achieve this it is essential that a person gets a good night's sleep which may vary from 6 to 8 hours depending upon the person. He should eat healthy and nuturitious food to take care of the requirements of his body and to ensure adequate energy levels in the body. If possible a vegetarian diet is better with a lot of greens. It is essential that a person does physical exercise such as walking for 45 minutes or some other aerobic exercise or plays games. In addition, a few yogic asanas, pranayam and mediation would definitely help in further increasing the overall focus and efficiency of a person and, thus, will enable him to give his best to the organization. Over-eating should be avoided as excess of anything is bad. As far as possible, there should be a balance in all that a person undertakes as too much exercise beyond the capacity of the body can also lead to fatigue.

All the above were practiced diligently by Dr. Sreedharan who used to get up at 4.30 am everyday followed by 30 minutes of meditation and about 30 minutes of yogic asanas and pranayam. In addition, he would walk for about 45 minutes at a brisk pace in the morning in summers which was changed to the evening in winter. Dr. Sreedharan used to read spiritual messages from the Bhagavad Gita and Srimad Bhagvatam which are ancient Indian texts giving us inspiring messages on how one should lead one's life. His diet was vegetarian and he would not even take milk products in his later years since milk was an extract from an animal. In the afternoon, after his lunch in the office Dr. Sreedharan would take a nap for about 15 minutes akin to a power nap which used to make him feel refreshed.

These good habits kept Dr. Sreedharan extremely fit till the age of 78 when the post pressures of the Zamrudpur accident and tight deadline of Phase-II took their toll leading to him suffering a heart attack. However, due to his past physical fitness he was able to recover very quickly from surgery after his by-pass and began monitoring the project again within ten days of his operation leading to successful completion of Phase-II.

The importance of good health and good habits was reinforced in the Delhi Metro's own Training Institute located at Shastri Park where all employees were trained. Yoga and meditation were a compulsory part of all the Foundation and initial courses attended by trainees and this was practiced between 4 pm to 5 pm on all working days. The habits gained in training were expected to become a part of the lifestyle of the employees later as it would help them in combating the day to day stresses of living and working. Metro jobs are quite stressful as the public expectations are quite high and the organization is responsible to the public directly.

> *Maintaining a positive mental attitude was essential in the face of multiple problems encountered during the construction of the Central Secretarait-Badarpur line including the Zamrudpur accident, hogging of spans, failure of the contractor, media pressure...*
>
> *Kumar Keshav, Director (Projects)*

■ He was waiting at the Delhi airport for his flight to Kolkata on Wednesday morning when he developed uneasiness. HT FILE

Sreedharan has a heart attack

HT Correspondent
■ htreporters@hindustantimes.com

NEW DELHI: Delhi metro chief E. Sreedharan (78) was admitted to New Delhi's Indraprastha Apollo Hospitals on Wednesday morning after he suffered a massive heart attack at the Delhi Airport.

The managing director of Delhi Metro Rail Corporation was about to board a flight to Kolkata at 6.30 a.m. when he developed uneasiness in the chest.

He was immediately taken to the medical centre at the airport, where he was stabilised before being rushed to Indraprastha Apollo Hospitals on Mathura Road.

"He was immediately investigated and is currently being managed for his ailment in the Coronary Intensive Care. A multidisciplinary team of doctors is monitoring his progress," said an Apollo spokesperson.

> **He is currently being managed in the Coronary Intensive Care. A multidisciplinary team of doctors is monitoring his progress.**
> APOLLO SPOKESMAN

A temporary pacemaker was implanted today to stabilize his heart.

The DMRD head has two blocked arteries and is undergoing treatment under senior cardiologist Dr S.K. Gupta.

Spirituality and Yoga are advocated among the employees of DMRC to lead a healthy and stress free life.

Steady Leadership

Whatever is to be done I do, but in reality I do not do anything.
- Yoga Vashishtha

In projects the frequent change of the top leader can be quite detrimental and in the DMRC, example of having a person like Dr. Sreedharan at the helm of affairs for 14 yrs. helped in maintaining continuity and accountability. However, the person who is chosen for the top position should be carefully picked with a proven track record and impeccable credentials. Frequent changes of the Chief Executive hampers the development of a proper vision and proper implementation as each person has his own style of leadership and every organization and its employees need stability as they also have to adjust to different leadership styles, attitudes and expectations. The leader should be a person with impeccable integrity with the ability to take bold and firm decisions. The decisions taken should be clear cut and should be transparent. The CEO should never appear to be a person who is taking sides with any particular group within the organization and should be impartial.

In DMRC the CEO had all these qualities and in addition he had a 'aura' which comes from a person who is spiritually enlightened. His magnetic power and strength worked as a battery and a power house through which other executives could draw inspiration and strength. Officers coming out of Dr. Sreedharan's room always came out feeling charged, motivated and fresh. Not only did he give clear cut decisions and solutions on every issue he had the unique ability to make every officer and every department feel as if they were the most important. He, thus, had good understanding of all the disciplines within DMRC and every one felt that he could go to him for guidance at all times. He also made himself easily accessible to the persons who played a key role in project implementation.

However, to be able to impart these high levels of energy and enthusiasm to his juniors, the CEO himself had to constantly work at keeping himself fully charged up. Thus, Dr. Sreedharan devoted almost three hours of his daily schedule to spiritual reading, meditation and yoga which were important inputs which he received daily to enable him to perform better. He had to pay careful attention to the fact that he should be careful about himself and he made a conscious effort not to allow power to go to his head. Therefore, behind the chair on which he used to sit in his office he had inscribed in metal the saying –"Whatever is to be done I do,

But in reality,

I do not do anything"

which he had taken from Yoga Vashistha. The above was very essential as Dr. Sreedharan had spent almost 20 years out of his 50 year career as the head of an organization-as Member Engineering of the Railway Board, Chairman-Managing Director of Konkan Railway and as the Managing Director of DMRC. In such top positions in any organization there is a natural tendency for psycophants and herd followers to hero worship and flatter the top man. This could be dangerous for CEOs as they may get influenced by interest groups who operate in many subtle ways. Thus, it is imperative that the CEO keeps his feet on the ground at all times. This was done successfully by Dr. Sreedharan by constantly reminding himself that whatever actions that were performed by him as a CEO were actually performed through him by a superior force or power with divine sanction. Therefore, it is important for all of us to remember that though it may appear that we have done a particular thing or achieved something spectacular but one should always remember that there is something hidden and divine which has made this possible.

> *As the MD was himself in his 70s and rarely took leave, employees felt reticent to take leave for fever, headaches, body aches and other common ailments.*

कार्यं करोमि न च किञ्चिदहं करो
Whatever to be done I do
but in reality,
I do not do anything.